THE
IDOLATRY
of
GOD

THE
IDOLATRY
of
GOD

BREAKING OUR ADDICTION
TO CERTAINTY AND SATISFACTION

PETER ROLLINS

HOWARD BOOKS
A DIVISION OF SIMON & SCHUSTER, INC.

NEW YORK   NASHVILLE   LONDON   TORONTO   SYDNEY   NEW DELHI

Howard Books
A Division of Simon & Schuster, Inc.
1230 Avenue of the Americas
New York, NY 10020

First Howard Books trade paperback edition January 2013

HOWARD and colophon are trademarks of Simon & Schuster, Inc.

For information about special discounts for bulk purchases,
please contact Simon & Schuster Special Sales at 1-866-506-1949
or business@simonandschuster.com.

The Simon & Schuster Speakers Bureau can bring authors to
your live event. For more information or to book an event contact
the Simon & Schuster Speakers Bureau at 1-866-248-3049 or
visit our website at www.simonspeakers.com.

Designed by Kyoko Watanabe

Manufactured in the United States of America

10 9 8 7 6 5 4 3 2 1

Library of Congress Cataloging-in-Publication Data

Rollins, Peter.
The idolatry of God : Breaking our addiction to certainty and satisfaction /
Peter Rollins.
p. cm.
1. Salvation—Christianity. 2. Christian life. I. Title.
BT752.R565 2012
243—dc232012008662

ISBN 978-1-4516-0902-8
ISBN 978-1-4516-0903-5 (ebook)

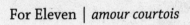

For Eleven | *amour courtois*

Contents

Contents

THE
IDOLATRY
of
GOD

The Apocalypse Isn't Coming, It Has Already Arrived

In popular religious literature, we find a deep fascination with the apocalypse. Millions have been made depicting the destruction of the world, the end times, and a war between the forces of good and evil that will usher in a new age.

These various depictions of the end seem to bask in a visceral and voyeuristic orgy of blood. Yet such reactionary views of the apocalypse, while seemingly ready to do away with everything, actually present an inherently conservative vision. For in destroying the world something fundamental is saved from the flames: namely, our desire for the perfect world.

In this vision of the apocalypse, the world that we inhabit is burnt up and replaced with a similar one that is only different from the present insomuch as it is a place where all our unfulfilled hopes and desires are finally satisfied. It is a world where that which we long for finally arrives. A world in which the sense of loss, pain, and unknowing that supposedly robs our life of pleasure is replaced with abundance, joy, and insight.

This new world is thought of as a place in which our current desires and longings find their ultimate fulfillment. What we hope for, dream about, and desire is not changed in any significant way—instead, our hopes, dreams, and desires are simply satisfied. In this way, everything is consumed in flames except for one thing: our desire for perfection. And so the main problem with these depictions of total destruction is not that they go too far, but that *they don't go far enough*.

> **The main problem with these depictions of total destruction is not that they go too far, but that *they don't go far enough*.**

Today the "Good News" of Christianity operates with much the same logic. It is sold to us as that which can fulfill our desire rather than as that which evokes a transformation in the very way that we desire. Like every other product that promises us fulfillment, Christ becomes yet another object in the world that is offered to us as a way of gaining insight and ultimate satisfaction. Jesus is thus presented as the solution to two interconnected problems: that we exist in a state of darkness concerning the meaning of the universe and that we are dissatisfied with our place within that universe.

The precise way that Jesus answers these problems is contested by different religious communities, and thus the way that Jesus is thought to provide a solution differs depending on whom one asks. History is overflowing with different portraits depicting the way that Jesus is the answer—Jesus the Marxist, Jesus the Capitalist, Jesus the meek, Jesus the mercenary, Jesus the social reformer, and Jesus the social conserver to name but a few. This enigmatic figure who died naked on a cross more than two thousand years ago has been clothed in various colorful ideological garments over the millennia.

When confronted with such a diverse and complex theological ecosystem, one full of differing and often competing images, one might despair of ever really working out how Jesus concretely answers these universal problems. With so many conflicting ideas, where is one to start? Did Jesus come to abolish religion or set up a new one? Did he seek to show us a way of escaping the world or of embracing it? Did he die to save us from our evil or did he die because our evil could not bear his presence? Did he even exist, and what is really known about him beyond the doctrinal claims of the church?

Over the ages various Christians have thrown their weight into these discussions, and we might be tempted to do the same. However, this book takes a different path, one that sees all these discussions as dangerous distractions that prevent us from touching upon the truly radical and revolutionary significance of Christ. For what if we cannot grasp the manner in which Christ is the solution to the problem of our darkness and dissatisfaction precisely because he *isn't* the solution? What if, instead of being the solution (i.e., the one who offers a way for us to gain certainty and satisfaction), he actually confronts us as *a problem*, a problem that places every attempt to find a solution for these ailments into question? To put this another way, what if Christ does not fill the empty cup we bring to him but rather smashes it to pieces, bringing freedom, not from our darkness and dissatisfaction, but freedom from our felt need to escape them?

It is the claim of this book that Christ signals a type of apocalyptic event much more dramatic than the one we find in fundamentalist literature. For in the figure of Christ we are confronted with an atomic event that does not destroy the world, but rather obliterates the way in which we exist within the world. In concrete terms, this means that the darkness and dissatisfaction that make their presence felt in our lives are not finally answered by certainty and satisfaction but are rather stripped of their weight and robbed of their sting.

In this way the new creation that arises in the aftermath of the Christ apocalypse is not "out there" but is a lived reality bubbling deep within. As Jesus once said, "The kingdom of God does not come with your careful observation, nor will people say, 'Here it is,' or 'There it is,' because the kingdom of God is within you." (Luke 17:20–21)

What follows then is an outline of what this proper apocalypse moment looks like. As such it is a work explicitly about the theme of salvation—not the type of salvation that is preached today from the pulpit, the false salvation that promises us freedom from our unknowing and dissatisfaction, but a salvation that takes places *within* our unknowing and dissatisfaction. One that directly confronts them, embraces them, and says "amen" to them.

> This book is about a salvation that takes places *within* our unknowing and dissatisfaction.

Part One

_____

THE OLD CREATION

CHAPTER 1

The Church Shouldn't Do Worship Music, the Charts Have It Covered

Creatio ex Nihilo

Whether we look at our own personal history or reflect upon the history of civilization, it is difficult to avoid the sense that we feel a lack in the very depths of our being, a lack that we try to cover over with any number of religious, political, and cultural remedies. This feeling might touch us like a breeze or knock us over with the force of a hurricane, but however it comes, most of us can testify to the feeling that there is something just beyond our reach that might help to fill this void, whether it is a person, money, power, possessions, God, or heaven.

It is natural for us to think that our present discontent arises as a result of something we currently do not have. We imagine there might be a way of abolishing the feeling if only we had the money, fame, job, or health that currently evades us. But people from all walks of life seem to experience the same kind of dissatisfaction that we do, even when they have the very things we believe would make our lives whole. And on the occasions when we gain the thing we believe will make us happy, we find that the satisfaction we experience is at best partial and at worst utterly unfulfilling.

In order to approach the root cause of this dissatisfaction and work out why it seems so difficult to abolish, let us begin by reviving an obscure and seemingly absurd Latin phrase that refers to the idea of something coming from nothing: *creatio ex nihilo*.

Upon first being confronted by this idea it might seem like nonsense, for how can nothing give rise to something? How can absence or lack be a generative and creative force in the world?

> How can absence or lack be a generative and creative force in the world?

Yet the idea of nothing bringing about something is not as strange as it might sound. Take the following example:

There was once a young woman who, late one evening, was taking a shower when the doorbell rang. Knowing that her husband was dozing in the upstairs bedroom she quickly wrapped herself in a towel and ran to the door. When she opened it, she was greeted by her next-door neighbor Joe.

Upon seeing her wearing nothing but a towel Joe pulled four hundred dollars from his back pocket, looked her in the eye, and said, "I have always been attracted to you. What do you say to the following indecent proposal? If I were to offer you this four hundred dollars right now, would you drop the towel for me?"

After a moment's reflection, she reluctantly agreed, dropped the towel, and let him look at her naked body. True to his word, Joe gave her the money and left.

Picking up the towel she hid the money and then went up to the bedroom. As she entered the room, her husband woke up and asked, "Did the doorbell ring a few minutes ago?"

"Oh yes," replied the woman. "It was just Joe from next door."

"Great! Did he give you the four hundred dollars he owes me?"

Here we witness a type of *creatio ex nihilo* at work, for the neighbor Joe has nothing to offer except the illusion of something (four hundred dollars that is not his), but this illusion generates a desired effect—the woman exposing her body. Nothing was made to look like something and created a result.

So how can this idea of nothing creating something

help us understand the dissatisfaction that seems so much a part of human life?

We Enter the World with Nothing

Infants undergo two births. The first is also the most plain to see—their physical entry into the world. The second, however, is less obvious; it is the birth of their self-consciousness. These two events occur close together, but they are not simultaneous, for their tiny bodies have already come onto the scene before they develop any real sense of being an individual. In this way their physical bodies are a type of womb out of which their selfhood arises.

Infants undergo two births.

This important point in human development was named "the mirror phase" by the psychoanalyst Jacques Lacan and is generally estimated to start between the ages of six to eighteen months. While the process is gradual, it is around this time that the infant begins to identify as existing in separation from her surroundings and slowly begins to experience herself as an individual.

The time before this awakening can be described as a type of prehistory, for it is the time before language, before self-consciousness, before the sense of "I." It is only as the infant begins to enter selfhood that her history really begins, a history that cannot articulate what came before it, yet which remains indelibly marked by it.

One of the fundamental experiences that arises from this second birth is a profound and disturbing sense of loss, for as soon as we experience our inner world, we encounter for the first time an outer world. As we develop a sense of our internal space, we are confronted with another one, a space existing beyond the borders of our flesh. Before the formation of our inner world, there is no sense of "me" and thus no notion of "you." There is no near and no far; no inside and, therefore, no outside; no barriers that would separate me from everything beyond the threshold of my skin. Before the advent of selfhood, the infant's body exists in a type of equilibrium with the environment, being impacted by it but not standing in contrast to it.

All this changes as the child gains a sense of selfhood, for at this point, the world is experienced as "out there." With the advent of the "I," there is an experience of that which is "not I." The sense of selfhood is marked indelibly with the sense of separation.

This means that one of our most basic and primal experiences of the world involves a sense of loss, for when we feel separated from something we assume that there was something we once had. The interesting thing to note, however, is that this sense of loss is actually an illusion, for we never actually lost anything. Why? Because there was no "me" before this experience of separation.

Before the experience of loss there was no self to have enjoyed the union that we sense has been ripped away from us. The very birth of our subjectivity then signals a sense of losing something that we never had in the first place.

This primordial experience of separation means nothing less than the experience of a gap, a feeling that there is some gulf between us and that which we have "lost." In light of this we can read the scriptural saying "For we brought nothing into the world" quite literally, as meaning that we enter the world with one thing in our possession: nothingness itself (i.e., a sense of some space separating us from the world we inhabit).

Horror Vacui

It is this sense of a gap that causes us to feel incomplete in some way. As a result, one of our first impulses is to find ways of abolishing the void. We attempt this by connecting our vague and abstract sense of separation to something concrete and then trying to gain it. Just as someone might manage what would otherwise be a crippling anxiety by coupling it with something particular (creating, for example, a fear of spiders), so we take our general sense of separation and connect it with an actual object that we might be able to gain. However, this strategy can never wholly work, as the disquieting sense of separation that makes its presence felt in our bodies has a hunger bigger than any object or objects could ever satisfy.

As we grow, the things we feed to this insatiable hunger change. As children we may think that a certain friendship, toy, or adventure will satisfy us, while as adults we might believe that a certain partner will fill the gap, or perhaps a job, a spiritual entity, a child, a political goal, or reaching a certain level of fame. The things that we believe will rid us of this gap differ and change over time, but the belief that something will fill the void remains constant.

Of course most of us will scoff at the idea there is something that will render us whole and will satisfy our seemingly insatiable desire. But what we deny with our lips is often found in the very texture of our lives. For instance, someone's hatred of the wealthy and famous is often little more than a sublimated form of jealousy. The very thing we say we hate in the other is often the very thing we desire most of all. Perhaps we feel unable to achieve such wealth, or we have been taught that it is morally wrong to do so. As such we have to turn our desire into a form of hatred, a hatred that masks what we really want. For instance, it is not uncommon to find small churches that speak disparagingly about larger communities, claiming that small is better. While this

> The very thing we say we hate in the other is often the very thing we desire most of all.

may sometimes reflect their true beliefs on the subject, one wonders if some of these churches would feel the same way if they began to grow significantly.

This mechanism is something we can see played out every day in school playgrounds across the world. Witness a little boy pulling the hair of a girl in his class—the only person who doesn't know that he really likes the girl is often the boy himself. What he denies with his words, however, is undermined by his actions.

An important distinction needs to be made at this point between objects that we seek because we feel (whether rightly or wrongly) that they will improve our life in some way and objects that we believe will fill the gap we experience at the very core of our existence. For example, one person may wish to make money in order to look after her family or gain some extra comfort, while someone else might pursue money in a way that suggests they think that wealth will provide them with ultimate meaning.

There is a very simple but vital mechanism that transforms an object from being something we would like to something we believe would make us whole: a prohibition. Whenever something we would like is refused to us in some way, this refusal causes us to want the object even more.

We can see this happening in a very transparent way while watching children play. We might imagine a child wanting to play with a toy he sees but is denied access to by a parent. By this act of prohibition, the child's normal desire for the object is transformed into something much more potent. He is likely to invest that toy with a significance not merited by the toy itself.

This prohibition was called "the Law" by the Apostle Paul. He understood that the prohibition of the Law does not cause one to renounce an object but rather fuels a self-destructive drive for it. This is a subject that we will take up in more detail in the following chapter.

I Need the Rabbit's Foot

Hollywood has made billions playing into this human experience of the gap, providing myths in which the lost object we believe will make us whole is finally gained. Film theorists call this lost object the MacGuffin, a term popularized by Alfred Hitchcock in the 1930s. The MacGuffin is a name that is given to whatever object helps drive the narrative forward, providing the necessary tension to keep an audience interested. The MacGuffin is that X for which some or all of the main characters are willing to sacrifice everything. In this way the object they seek is more than something they want in order to make their lives a little better; it is something that evokes in them an obsessive form of desire. The object might take the form of money, fame, victory, power, a man, or a woman. The point is not what actually fills the role of the MacGuffin, but that there is something that has that role, something that people want in some excessive way. It is the object for which everything will be sacrificed, the object that seems to promise fulfillment, satisfaction, and lasting pleasure.

One particularly interesting example of a MacGuffin in action can be seen in J. J. Abrams's film *Mission: Impossible III*. For here the director hints at the MacGuffin's utterly contingent nature.

The entire movie revolves around a mysterious object called the Rabbit's Foot. All the main players in the movie desperately seek this object, and yet at no point do we ever learn exactly what the Rabbit's Foot actually is. This is brought home most clearly in one scene where a technician working for the IMF (Impossible Missions Force) christens this enigmatic object of desire with the name "Anti-God"—a name that gives us a glimpse into the very nature of the MacGuffin. For if God is understood as the source of everything, then the name "Anti-God" brings to mind nothingness itself.

By refusing to give the object any real content, *Mission: Impossible III* hints at the provisional and ultimately superfluous nature of the MacGuffin. The movie shows how it acts as a type of void, a void that produces all the conflict and desire. It is a nothing that produces everything. It is *creatio ex nihilo* in action.

In reality, the movie does give the impression that the Rabbit's Foot has some positive content when it implies that the black market arms dealer knows what it is. What might have made the movie more intellectually satisfying would have been a final twist, one where we discover that the only reason the arms dealer is so obsessed with possessing the Rabbit's Foot is because he mistakenly thinks the Impossible Missions Force wants it. In this way the Rabbit's Foot could have existed in the movie as a pure fabrication without any specific content, a nothing that gains its significance purely through a misunderstanding.

In life we find ourselves pursuing various MacGuffins—impotent things we falsely believe will make us whole. What we see in the structure of Hollywood movies is but a clear reflection of this structure. And just as Hollywood movies generally hide the impotence of what we seek, so our dreams and fantasies do the same—ultimately covering over the fact that what we think will satisfy our souls is really powerless to do so.

> **In life we find ourselves pursuing various MacGuffins—impotent things we falsely believe will make us whole.**

The Originality of Original Sin

This idea of a gap at the core of our being has an ancient theological name: Original Sin. Unfortunately this term has all but lost its depth and credibility due to its misuse by the church today. But if we consider Original Sin in its most literal definition, we can begin to appreciate how it refers to a primal separation—for "sin" means separation, and "original" refers to that which comes first. In this way Original Sin is simply the ancient theological name given to the experience that we have outlined above. It is a phrase that refers to the feeling of gap that marks us all from the very beginning.

We have seen how this nothing at the core of our being causes us to imagine something that might fill it, something that would make us whole. But this belief in something that would finally bring satisfaction is nothing more than a fantasy we create, a fantasy that fuels the obsessive drive we have for books, talks, and people who promise a life of total sexual, emotional, and/or spiritual fulfillment. This Original Sin is the very thing that causes us to falsely think it is not original at all. This sense of gap makes us think that there must have been something before it, an original blessing that we somehow lost.

Sadly, almost the entire existing church fails to embrace the full radicality of what Original Sin actually means, for they presuppose that there is something we are separated from, something that will bring wholeness and insight.

This is witnessed in one of its most raw forms in contemporary worship music. There is today a profound similarity between popular music and the music that is being created by contemporary worship bands. Often the two are almost indistinguishable, the only difference between them being the object they hold up as the meaning of existence.

Both operate with the same structure in that both affirm some object (a particular woman or man, fame, sex, money, God, or revenge) as that which evokes our desire and deserves our devotion. Some object is thus claimed to be the answer to the profound lack that we experience at the core of our being.

The logic of popular music is profoundly attractive to much of the contemporary church because the charts are full of worship songs created by a multibillion-dollar industry, and while this industry is not interested in holding up the religious idea of God as the ultimate answer, it is very interested in exploiting the human desire to hold something up as the ultimate answer. It is then a simple matter for Christian bands to swap Jesus for whatever object a particular song sets up as the ultimate answer. Indeed, it is not uncommon for church music groups to go further than simply copying the logic of contemporary pop music, going so far as to take specific songs and changing a few of the words so that they point to a different love object. This technique attempts to gain some credibility from people like Luther, Charles Wesley, and William Booth, all of whom based some of their hymns on the popular tunes of the day. Is it any wonder that musicians like Ray Charles returned the favor, basing some of their most popular music on old gospel songs? The issue is not which came first, sacred worship music or the more secular kind, but the fact that in both the church and the charts today we find the same style of music: one that holds up some object as the highest principle around which our life should revolve.

Sell Church

If we take the idea that contemporary worship music holds up some X as the highest good that we desire, seek, pursue, and adore with all our might, then it starts to become clear that worship music is ubiquitous today. The menu is of course varied, with a whole range of things being placed on the throne before which we worship, but the throne remains intact throughout. Each worship song points to something that implicitly or explicitly promises to fill the gap we feel piercing the heart of our being.

> Each worship song points to something that implicitly or explicitly promises to fill the gap we feel piercing the heart of our being.

When such music is used in a church context, it renders the source of faith into just one more product promising us fulfillment, happiness, and unwavering bliss. The church then takes its place beside every other industry that is in the business of selling satisfaction. Religious hymns become little more than advertising jingles, and the clergy come to resemble slick salespeople presenting their god-product to the potential consumer.

In daily life we are confronted with a vast array of voices telling us that we can be happy, fulfilled, and content only if we adopt a particular lifestyle, buy a particular product, or look a particular way. Everywhere we turn we are being promised that our life can be wonderful if we follow a certain formula. It is as if the world is a huge vending machine full of products, each one promising to satisfy our soul.

But instead of offering a freedom from this type of thinking, the church has simply joined the party and placed its own product into the machine. Their god-product takes its place alongside all the other things vying for our attention with their promises to fill the gap in our lives and render our existence meaningful. Take one or mix and match: luxury car, financial success, fame, or Jesus; they all pretty much promise the same satisfaction.

This idea of God as the fulfillment of our desires is so all-pervasive today that most of us take it for granted. Whether people accept the idea of God or reject it, they seem to be talking about the same thing: a being who satisfies our soul by filling the gap in our existence. The only conflict is that some people reject this god-product as fiction while others accept it.

A God by Any Other Name Would Smell as Sweet

The particular object we postulate as the way of filling the gap we experience in our lives is irrelevant. It may be success, good looks, money, Jesus, children, a partner, or even stamp collecting. It is whatever we act toward as if it were the thing that would rid us of our sense of emptiness. It is that seductive object that seems to address us with a promise: "I can make you whole and complete if only you would come to me." Yet, as with the Sirens of Greek mythology, heeding this call, as we shall see, always ends in wanton destruction.

CHAPTER 2

On Not Getting What You Want, and Liking It

Birth of the Idol

On the level of human existence, we are marked from the very beginning by a sense of loss/separation/nothing that creates in us the belief in something that can fill up the void and make us satisfied. While different people and cultures will have different understandings of what this filler might be, we are all marked by it and driven by it.

In the same way that theological language has a name for this sense of gap at the heart of our being—Original Sin—it also has a name for the imaginary object that we believe will fill this gap: the Idol. In a basic sense, an Idol can be understood as that object which we believe is the answer to all our problems, that thing we believe can fill the fundamental gap we experience festering in the very depths of our human experience.

What we learn here is that the terms "Original Sin" and "Idolatry" are totally interconnected. The sense of separation we feel causes us to imagine some object that would take the feeling away, and this is the Idol.

An Idol is not an Idol because of some property a particular object has; it is an Idol because we project an absolute value onto it. For instance, one person may wish to keep fit in order to look and feel more healthy, while another might keep fit because he thinks it will somehow make him complete. One person might have a child because she loves the idea of bringing someone into the world, while another looks to having a child because she somehow thinks that this will plug up the dissatisfaction in her existence. It is the latter approach that renders keeping fit or having a child into an Idol. The supposed X that makes a person or thing an Idol is itself a nothing, a misperception. For one person wealth might be a way of making life a little easier, while for another it is nothing less than a god.

What we see taking place in the church today is the reduction of God to an Idol, that is, to a thing that will satisfy us and fill the gap we feel in our hearts. In thinking of God in this way, the church ends up mimicking every other industry by claiming that they can take away the sense of loss that marks our life. In this way, they make

God into nothing more than an impotent MacGuffin. By misunderstanding the nature of faith, they turn the good news of Christianity into the bad news of Idol worship. By claiming that God is the way to fill this gap, they reduce the divine to the level of a product.

It is no coincidence then that Sin and Idolatry are two overriding concerns in the Hebrew scriptures. For these are as intimately intertwined as the Law and transgression. Just as the apostle Paul writes of the

> **What we see taking place in the church today is the reduction of God to an Idol.**

Law generating our desire for that which it prohibits (thus holding us captive to the very thing it condemns), so Original Sin is that which generates our desire for (and creation of) the Idol, ensuring that we remain forever within its orbit.

In contrast to the obscure, moralistic, and esoteric definitions that terms such as "Original Sin" and "Idolatry" generally evoke in religious settings, we can see that they can actually be employed to name very real phenomena that all of us deeply know and experience. Original Sin can be understood very simply as the sense of loss that all humans experience in the process of coming to self-awareness, while Idolatry refers to any object that we imagine can fill this inner void. To put it another way, we mistakenly feel that we have lost something central to our humanity (Original Sin) and then postulate some object we believe will restore what we have lost, something we believe will bring wholeness and fulfillment to our lives (the Idol). In this way the two terms are intimately interwoven, for without Original Sin there would be no Idolatry. Without the formation of the gap at the moment of self-awareness, we would not be provoked into imagining something that could fill it. Original Sin thus opens up the possibility of Idolatry.

Our Inability to Get the Idol Creates the Idol

It is not enough to claim that Original Sin leads to the creation of Idols. For the creation of an Idol, one more element is required—something we have touched on previously. In order to approach what this second ingredient is, let's return to an example of how desire functions in everyday life. Let us imagine that a child wishes to play with a toy that some other child has. At first she may only have a passing interest in the object; however, if the one who is holding the object refuses to let her play with it, the object can begin to take on a greater significance. Here we witness how the inability to get the toy actually fuels the child's interest in having the toy. She will likely become much more interested in the object that moments before had only a passing appeal. If the child who has the toy continues to prohibit it, this denial can invest the toy with a magical quality for the first child. Here, the "no" uttered by the one with the toy acts as the catalyst for transforming a cheap plastic object into something sublime.

We can see this wonderfully expressed in Lacan's reflections concerning a thought experiment forwarded by Immanuel Kant in his *Critique of Practical Reason*. Kant imagines that a man has the opportunity to sleep with a woman whom he desires. However, should he spend the night with her, the very next day he shall be hung on a gallows. For Kant, the decision concerning what to do is simple: the man should, for purely rational and self-interested reasons, refuse. Lacan, however, employing and developing the insights of Freud, showed how the very existence of an obstacle (here the gallows) can not only be ineffective in stopping us from pursuing something, but can actually be the very thing that invests something with an imaginary quality that evokes excessive, obsessional desire in us. It is then the gallows that invests the object of our desire with its seductive, Idolatrous *je ne sais quoi*.

It is this very structure that the apostle Paul was referring to in his famous writings on the Law and sin. While people tended to think that the Law and sin existed at opposite ends of a spectrum—the Law being the thing that defended us against sin—Paul writes of how they actually are intertwined and exist on the same side. For Paul, the Law is the "no" that appears to be opposed to the very structure it actually creates and upholds.

In light of this, we can begin to appreciate how the experience of separation that marks our birth as self-conscious beings (Original Sin) must be combined with a prohibition (the Law) in order to create the idea of something that will satisfy us and make us complete (the Idol).

Our first experience of this "no" occurs as infants when we experience a separation from our mother's breast. During the weaning process, the child's access to the breast is blocked. The infant discovers that he cannot have what he wants. It is at this point that what he cannot have takes on a symbolic significance beyond the mere satisfaction of a need. In other words, the "no" that we are confronted with—the Law—turns what was previously an object that satisfies basic needs into an object of veneration.

> **The "no" that we are confronted with—the Law—turns what was previously an object that satisfies basic needs into an object of veneration.**

From that time forth we become little industries dedicated to the creation of Idols.

"The End" Is Not the End

If Original Sin is the experience of primal separation, then the Law can be called the force of alienation, for it appears to block access to that magical thing that will make us whole while really creating it (taking a normal object and causing us to see it as the answer to all our problems). It is this combination of separation and alienation that together provides the essential ingredients for the creation of the Idol.

Original Sin and the Idol

This Idolatry goes on to mark our entire existence, touching every part of our lives. This concept is captured in the often misunderstood notion of Total Depravity— a phrase that does not mean there is no good within us, but instead refers to the idea that there is no part of our existence that is not marked by and influenced by the effect of this separation and alienation. It festers within us as we grow; the only thing that changes is the type of Idol we bow before.

To understand this a little better, let us imagine three brothers who gain a small inheritance and who each wish to use it in order to make ten million dollars. The first sets up a business that struggles from the very beginning. In the midst of the difficulties he meets a woman whom he subsequently marries. By the time they have their first child, he has to put his dream of making ten million dollars to one side in order to secure a job with a steady income. He thus gives up on his dream, yet his dream remains in the back of his mind as the thing that he had to renounce. When times are good, the loss of this dream is barely felt, but when he is arguing with his wife or having difficulties at work, he often comes to resent the path he has chosen, feeling that perhaps he lacked the courage to pursue what he really wanted.

The second brother begins in much the same way as the first, setting up a business that ultimately fails. Unperturbed by this, he continues to pursue his goal by establishing new ventures that never quite work. In pursuing his goal, he forsakes the possibility of a life partner, uses people as a means to an end, and suffers from stress-related ill health. Yet, no matter the personal cost, he continues to pursue his dream, even though it becomes evident to all around him that he has sacrificed too much and will likely never achieve what he really wants.

In contrast, the third brother has a lot more success. He invests his inheritance in a number of small companies that grow rapidly. With the returns he makes he goes on to invest wisely in other firms until he reaches his original goal: ten million dollars. At first, he is elated. He is able to buy the car he always wanted and live in the house he has dreamed of. He takes a couple of luxury holidays and tries out some expensive recreational activities. Yet there is within him a growing sense of dis-ease. Is this it? Is this what it feels like to be happy and complete? He gets what he believes will make him happy, and while he is more comfortable than he used to be, the emptiness in his soul is still there. Indeed it is more pronounced than ever, because what he thought would fill the void did no such thing. "Perhaps," he thinks to himself, "what I really need is one hundred million dollars."

Each of the brothers experiences a certain amount of pleasure. The first experiences the pleasure of better relationships, a lack of stress, and more recreation time.

The second brother feels the pleasure that comes from the single-minded pursuit of a goal, with all the fantasies that entails. The third brother gains the pleasure of being able to buy many things that will make his life easier and more comfortable.

But the problem is that the dream of having ten million dollars as a means of being finally happy is oppressive to each of them. Each brother is confronted with a fundamental pain that prevents him from enjoying the pleasure he receives (having better relationships, seeking a goal, or having wealth). The first brother stops trying to achieve his goal because of the obstacles (the Law) and has to settle for less than he desires; the second tries unsuccessfully to break through the obstacles and continues to smash up against impossible odds, while the third brother overcomes the obstacles only to find that the ten million dollars is ultimately unfulfilling. Here we witness how the Original Sin/Law/Idolatry matrix ensures that the life these brothers live is laced with a sense of failure, emptiness, and impotence.

Each path to what they believe will make them complete leaves them lacking in some way. Renunciation of the goal, the refusal to relinquish it, and the attainment of it all have their shadow side.

It is this truth that

> **The Original Sin/Law/Idolatry matrix ensures that the life they live is laced with a sense of failure, emptiness, and impotence.**

is obscured in so many Hollywood movies. What we see played out again and again is a situation in which the protagonist actually gets what he or she wants above all else—the kiss, the money, the bad guy, etc. However, we rarely see what happens after the hero grasps what is sought, for if we did, the impotence of the MacGuffin would be revealed and we would not get the feel-good fantasy of fulfillment that so much popular cinema offers. For example, a romantic film might end with a passionate kiss that symbolizes the beginning of a new relationship between two people who fought all obstacles to be together. It will not end with a scene that depicts the same couple, one year later, sitting uncomfortably in a restaurant, silently resenting each other because of some unresolved domestic issue.

This is something that *Austin Powers* brilliantly exposes in a scene where the villains laugh maniacally because they believe that they have secured one hundred billion dollars (the thing that they want more than anything else). However, instead of the standard cutaway in which we would be left with an image of the excessive pleasure that these people are receiving, the scene continues to focus on the villains. After a little while the excessive laughing dies down, and we see that the characters start to feel a little embarrassed at their over-the-top hysterics. Soon the laughter ends, and they exit the scene in a sheepish, embarrassed way. The scene gains its comic effect by exposing the logic that we all know is true and yet disavow or repress: that the excessive pleasure we imagine receiving from what we want most of all is fleeting at best.

The reason narratives in which the protagonist finds the Idol have such power and popularity is the way that they play on the deepest part of our psyche. They bring to light our own sense of incompleteness, reflect it back to us, and then provide us with the pleasure of seeing this lack fulfilled in the lives of the actors we identify with. Indeed, the structure is further supported by the fantasy that these actors have achieved their Idol in real life as well as in their cinematic roles.

This structure is explored in an interesting way in Clint Eastwood's adaptation of Robert James Waller's bestselling novel *The Bridges of Madison County*. The movie focuses upon a brief but intense and passionate affair between a woman named Francesca and a photographer named Robert Kincaid who happens to be passing through the town where Francesca lives. Francesca is married with two children, and while her husband is a good man, she is lonely and bored with her lot as a housewife in a small town. This boredom is latent in her but comes to the surface when she encounters the independent and free-spirited photographer who brings this dissatisfaction to light and offers glimpses of a more exciting and carefree existence.

One of the movie's central tensions arises in the palpable and inevitable conflict that the affair creates in her life. In the four days she has with Robert, she feels a certain guilt while also being enlivened by a new sense of desire and longing. Her body is alive, perhaps for the first time, with passions, dreams, and desires that have previously been dormant.

The movie then circles around the question of what she should do in light of this encounter with someone who seems to offer her everything she could want. Should she return to the life she had before the affair or run away and risk everything for her new love? Here Francesca faces the problem of whether to abandon her happy but ultimately unfulfilling family life and pursue what she senses might fulfill her emotionally, sexually, and intellectually; or return to her family life, where she can find many small, secondary, and ultimately paltry pleasures.

For Francesca, her current life eventually wins out, and she renounces the pursuit of the mysterious and alluring photographer. The suggestion is that she knows that her desire to be with the photographer is ultimately a fantasy that would lead to disaster if pursued—after all, he is already divorced, is always on the move, and loves to be alone.

And yet she is unable to completely move on, living with a memory of her lover that is tinged with the pleasure and pain of a palpable longing. She may have forsaken her potential for fulfillment, but she never forgets.

The undying and unconditional nature of her longing is expressed powerfully when, after her death, Francesca's daughter finds the will that asks for her ashes to be scattered where Robert's ashes were scattered some years before. In this way, her drive for Robert seems to exist even beyond the grave, continuing to resound after both have passed away.

In this way *The Bridges of Madison County* reflects back to us a reality that we all face—the conflict between giving up what we long for or pursuing it only to find pain.

> **This is the impossible situation we all face— the conflict between giving up what we long for or pursuing it only to find that it does not provide us with what we imagined.**

The Other Has the Happiness That I Seek

Belief in the Idol is not only destructive because it causes us to pursue something that will not ultimately satisfy us, it is also destructive because it can put us into conflict with others whom we believe have actually gained the satisfaction that eludes us. One of the primary fuels for hatred of others is the fantasy that they have access to the pleasure that we unsuccessfully seek. While the Idol is impossible for us to grasp, we imagine that others have been successful in getting it, and we can hate them for it.

Take the example of ministers standing in front of their congregation preaching passionately against the sexual sin of people in their city, working themselves into a sweat about the orgies, sex parties, and deviant behavior going on just beyond the walls of the church. It is not hard to see how often all this pent-up emotion and moral indignation is nothing more than a thin veil hiding the truth that these ministers are jealous of all the fun the "sinners" are having. The people "out there" are having so much pleasure; they have the Idol that we do not.

This can also be seen to play out when someone breaks up with us. It is not uncommon to imagine that the other person is out partying, meeting new people, and generally having a ball. All the while we might be unhappy, unstable, and unable to leave the house. The one who left appears to have the pleasure that we lack and we resent him for it, even wishing her harm. More than this, we are willing to hurt ourselves in order to rob her of her pleasure (the most extreme form being suicide—where we will end our own life to cause the other a crippling guilt).

We see how we imagine the other having the satisfaction we do not in the famous biblical story in which King Solomon is asked to resolve a dispute between two young women who both declare that they are the mother of a young child (1 Kings 3:16–28). One woman claims that the other woman's child died during the night and that she then swapped the dead child with her living infant of roughly the same age. The other woman denies it, and so King Solomon is charged with ascertaining who the true mother is.

After deliberating on the case, Solomon calls for a

sword and declares that the living son should be cut into two pieces, with each woman receiving half. As the judgment is pronounced, the true mother screams out, "Please, my lord, give her the live child—do not kill him!" In contrast, the liar responded, "It shall be neither mine nor yours—divide it!" At this point Solomon knows who the real mother of the child is and gives the baby to her. For it is obvious that the real mother would seek to protect her child at all costs.

In this story we see firsthand how hatred of the other gaining what we believe we cannot have works. The woman who had experienced the death of her own child would rather see the child murdered than witness her neighbor have what she believed would make her whole and happy (the child). This is more than the horrific pain that must come from the loss of a child; this is an example of how our own sense of losing what we imagine would have made us whole can cause us to despise those who we imagine have it. In light of this, we can appreciate the ancient parable of the farmer who is visited by an angel who says, "God has seen how faithful you have been over the years and wishes to give you a blessing. Ask for one thing, and it will be given to you." Just as the farmer is about to speak, the angel interrupts: "Wait, this is indeed a great day, for the blessing is even better than that. Not only will God give you whatever you want, he will give your neighbor double." The farmer pauses for a moment, then points at his eyes: "Then take one of these."

If we cannot have the Idol, then we wish to prevent

the other from having it. We take pleasure in taking from the other what she does not actually have, even if it means taking something from ourselves.

So then, not only is this Idol oppressive because we can never seem to grasp it; it is also oppressive because we think others have grasped it.

Another way that the Idol proves destructive lies in the way we often pretend to have that which makes us whole and satisfied in order to evoke the admiration, desire, or jealousy of others. For instance, a woman in a destructive and unfulfilling relationship with someone who is highly respected or admired in society might continue to date him because she gets a form of pleasure from people looking at her and wishing they were in her position (even though the reality of her position is awful). Or perhaps a family that is falling apart on the inside sends yearly Christmas letters to friends and family describing how wonderful their children are and how well they are doing. While the children might be unholy terrors, there can be a certain type of substitute satisfaction from projecting out an image of being satisfied. In both of these examples, the pleasure one receives is not gained from actually *having* something satisfying but rather in imagining how other people might think that one does.

The fantasy that there is an ultimate satisfaction fuels conflict through our imagining that another has achieved the pleasure we cannot or through our pretending that we have it. Such things can be used to galvanize individuals to distrust, dislike, and hate a different community. The Idol destroys not simply by breaking us from within (being crushed by our inability to ever grasp it) but also by breaking us apart from one another.

> The fantasy that there is an ultimate satisfaction fuels conflict through our imagining that another has achieved the pleasure we cannot.

A Life of Sin

Within this framework of Original Sin, the Law, and Idolatry, we can come to a proper understanding of the theological term "sin." Within this framework, sinful acts are simply acts dedicated to helping us grasp the ever elusive Idol. Sinful activities thus have no necessary connection with a particular act like drinking, drug use, or sexual promiscuity. Rather, sinful activities are whatever we do with the goal of bringing us into proximity with that which we believe will fill the void in our existence. This means that a sinful activity could involve anything from drug abuse, sex, and alcohol to charitable work, marriage, church attendance, prayer and random acts of kindness. If an act is designed to bridge the gap between Original Sin and the Idol, then it falls into the theological category known in the biblical text as "works."

There are a famous set of diagrams that have found

their way into different religious tracts over the years that attempt to capture visually how our separation from God works. According to the first diagram, we stand on one side of a great chasm and God stands on the other.

For these tracts, there are various ways in which we attempt to cross this chasm, but none of them work.

In contrast, the Cross is shown to fill the gap. All we need to do is accept Christ, and the gap between ourselves and God will be bridged.

What is interesting here is the way that these diagrams offer a solid visual description of the problem we have been describing thus far: we feel separated from that which will make us complete, and our various attempts at bridging the gap inevitably fail.

However, instead of seeing Christ as the apocalyptic destruction of this whole approach, these diagrams see Jesus as a more effective way to bridge the gap. These diagrams thus obscure the truth by calling the Idol "God." In this way, the contemporary understanding of "God" is nothing more than a mask worn by the Idol.

Avoiding the Truth

Because so much of the church has bought into the idea that Jesus is the ultimate bridge between ourselves and that which we feel separated from, it finds itself with the same problem as any other company that promises a product that will make you happy: how to hide the reality that it doesn't really work.

There are a number of different ways to solve this problem. The first is the strategy of *deferment*—convincing the individual that he is not getting the satisfaction he was promised because he is doing something wrong. This strategy emphasizes techniques to help you step into the wholeness that you supposedly already have. In terms of Christianity, one is invited to attend conferences, read the latest book, pray more, read the Bible more, worship more, ad infinitum. The reason you don't feel like you have crossed the chasm is because there is something you need to do first, some supplement is required.

The second technique is that of *repression*, where we are encouraged to ignore what we know. This works particularly well when people are deeply invested in the lie. At a certain point, it is psychologically easier to pretend to yourself that you are happy than admit that very little has changed. The difference between deferment and repression is that in the former, you know you are not fulfilled but you think you are doing something wrong, while in the latter you know you are not fulfilled but pretend to yourself that you are.

> It is psychologically easier to pretend to yourself that you are happy than admit that very little has changed.

We can understand repression if we take the example of debates concerning secrecy and the state. These generally revolve around the question of what information should be available to the public and what information needs to remain hidden. But this debate can obscure the most powerful aspect of groups dedicated to revealing secrets (such as WikiLeaks). Instead of the liberal claim that WikiLeaks is important because it tells the public things it does not know, the philosopher Slavoj Žižek has pointed out that its true power lies in telling us things we already know but refuse to acknowledge.

Of course WikiLeaks tells us lots of things that most of us had no idea about (what certain diplomats thought of a particular leader and so on). However, the information that has caused the most disruption has related to such things as unlawful arrests, black hole prisons, torture, and the murder of innocents—all things that a large number of us already knew was happening. The difference was that before the revelations we were able to engage in plausible deniability. As long we are not confronted with the direct evidence, we can refuse to know what we know; to put it in another way, we can refuse to acknowledge what we are already aware of. It is not so much that we now know, but rather that now we know that we know.

This same logic is what we see played out in our personal lives, as well—in a marriage, for example, where someone ignores the obvious infidelity of his partner. While it might be clear that one partner is having an affair, everything can continue as long as it is not directly said. In this way, the knowledge is ignored. The problem is that repressed knowledge always finds a way to express itself. What we repress will make its presence felt in some way, such as in anger, self-harm, or depression.

Another strategy in addition to deferment and repression is *disavowal*. Here a person does not even accept the reality of his or her situation, but ignores it entirely. This is different than repression in a subtle but clear way. Let us return to the above example of a partner who is obviously having an affair. Once the facts are presented, the person who is repressing the knowledge will feel angry (rather than surprised) at being shown what he or she already knew. But the person who has disavowed the evidence will simply refuse to accept it.

Each of these strategies—deferral, repression, and disavowal—is employed by us to avoid a confrontation with the truth: our lives are not fulfilled; we are still seeking things in addition to our religious commitments; our religious beliefs have not provided us what they seemed to promise.

The Idol Exists and Is Sublime and Meaningful

From all of this we can isolate three characteristics of the Idol—characteristics that are important to understand at this point so that later on we might contrast them with the notion of God as revealed in Christianity.

The first thing we can say about the Idol is that we experience it as *existing*. Indeed, not only does it exist, it often feels like the only thing that does exist. To exist means to stand out, to be able to be grasped in some tangible, concrete way, such as through thought, sight, smell, or touch. The Idol's existence can seem so overwhelming that most other things lose their importance and fade away into the background. Of course, most of the time we do not experience it in such an intense way, but the closer we are to it, the more its existence pushes other things into the background. In truth, however, the Idol doesn't exist; it is a false construct that is often revealed as fiction only once we think we have grasped it. When we get the thing we believe will make us whole, we discover that it is just a normal object with no magical powers to fill the gap in our being.

Second, the Idol is felt to be *sublime;* it stands out as the most tantalizing and beautiful of all things. The more powerful the hold of this Idol, the more its beauty eclipses every-

> When we get the thing we believe will make us whole, we discover that it is just a normal object with no magical powers to fill the gap in our being.

thing else. Again the truth is actually the very opposite, for if we ever grasp the Idol, we discover that it is nothing more than a form of fool's gold, having only the appearance of value.

Finally, the Idol strikes us as that which is ultimately *meaningful*. Indeed, we can become so obsessed with the Idol that it seems to be the only thing in the world that *is* meaningful. We are tethered to it and revolve around it. Everything else pales into insignificance when compared to the Idol that holds us in its thrall. Once more, however, the reality is that the Idol only appears to have meaning. For in grasping the object, we are confronted with the truth that ultimate meaning does not reside there.

Out of Nothing Arises the False God

While these seemingly arcane theological terms (Original Sin, the Law, and Idolatry) can strike us as obscurantist, they are actually, if understood properly, descriptive of some very basic aspects of our lived reality—a reality of which we are generally not aware.

Over the centuries, however, these terms have become encrusted with so many additional meanings that it is difficult for us to see them in their purity and precision. But we must resist blindly accepting the meanings we have heard preached from Sunday school to the pulpit. The more obscure the meanings we place on these terms, the more meaningless and useless they become.

By seeing how these three terms are interwoven, we

can begin to understand the phrase *creatio ex nihilo* in a much more radical way. Traditionally the term was used as a way of saying that God creates out of nothing; however, now we can perceive a deeper meaning, one much more basic and true to our human experience: out of nothing (Original Sin), a god is created (the Idol). Not just any god, but a god-product that promises so much and delivers so little. The god-product that we are encouraged to buy into and place at the center of our lives. So when we hear the term *creatio ex nihilo*, we can turn its original meaning around and see how out of nothing a god arises—the religious god, the false god that prevents us from discovering the apocalyptic notion of God testified to in the figure of Christ.

For instead of God being that which fills the gap at the core of our being, we shall soon discover something much more amazing and liberating: namely that the God testified to in Christianity exposes the gap for what it is, obliterates it, and invites us to participate in an utterly different form of life, one that brings us beyond slavery to the Idol.

CHAPTER 3

Hiding Behind the Mask
That We Are

Breaking the Fifth Wall

One of the most influential and successful TV detective shows of all time is *Miami Vice*. The show revolves around the undercover work of two detectives, Sonny Crockett (Don Johnson) and Ricardo Tubbs (Philip Michael Thomas), as they investigate various crime rings and arrest the villains.

Over the years, the show explored numerous themes, but one of the most interesting plots came in the final episode of season four. In this episode, Sonny Crockett narrowly escapes death by jumping off the boat of a drug dealer moments before it explodes. We discover that he is still alive when the scene cuts to a makeshift hospital room where Crockett lies in a coma. It turns out that he is being given private medical attention by a powerful drug lord who wants to know who blew up the boat.

After a few days Crockett gradually regains consciousness, but his memory of events is fragmented, and he has trouble remembering who he is. Because he is surrounded by criminals, he is constantly being treated as if he were Sonny Burnett—his undercover alias. Crockett thus begins to recall his undercover persona and identify directly with it. Although Sonny Burnett is nothing but a fiction constructed by the Miami Police Department in order to infiltrate criminal gangs, Crockett now takes it as a description of who he is. He so identifies with this fictional persona that he even shoots his best friend and work colleague Ricardo Tubbs in an alleyway. It is only after this that cracks in Crockett's self-perception begin to appear—not directly, but via a turbulent dream that betrays an unconscious wrestling with his new identity and with what he has done.

What we witness here is that Sonny Crockett fully identifies, at a conscious level, with a false story that was constructed for him by his police department. Sonny Burnett is nothing more than an elaborate fabrication, but because of the coma, Crockett believes that this false persona defines who he is. He so closely identifies with this false identity that it influences how he behaves, causing him to do things that would have been unthinkable to him before. Yet, in the midst of this, something is disturbing him at an unconscious level, a feeling that disturbs the smooth running of his new life and hints at the true status of the story he tells himself about himself. His waking life involves a type of repression in which he avoids confronting a truth that is expressed in his dreams.

What we witness in this storyline is that Crockett embraces his false identity as true (consciously) and yet is disturbed by this embrace at an unconscious level. We witness him as a split subject, at war with himself.

> We witness Crockett as a split subject, at war with himself.

While the show suggests that this detective is really Sonny Crockett, the truth, of course, is that Sonny Crockett is fictional. A character created by a group of writers that is played by the actor Don Johnson. A reality that the show cannot expose, as it would destroy our suspension of disbelief.

There are, however, programs that do expose the fictional nature of the characters in them—a technique that was used in the 1980s show *Moonlighting*, a series that often had the characters stare straight into the camera and say something that directly addressed the audience. This technique meant that the viewer was confronted with the fictional nature of what they were watching. This jarring technique, used in French New Wave cinema, is known as "breaking the fourth wall." The "fourth wall" is considered to be an invisible barrier that stands between the actors and the spectators. To experience the breaking of the fourth wall means that we are directly confronted with the fictional nature of whatever production we are watching. But the breaking of the fourth wall stops short of confronting us with a deeper reality: that *we* are fictional characters.

The drug dealer Burnett is a fictional character being played by Crockett who is himself a fictional character being played by Johnson. But Johnson is also a fictional character, not simply because of the way such a star is presented to the public, but because all the stories we tell ourselves about ourselves have a fictional quality.

The fictional nature of our identity is not made obvious in the mundane details of our daily life, but in those moments when the story we affirm begins to crack. When we act "out of character," we are doing exactly that, manifesting something that cannot be adequately explained or contained within the story we directly identify with. This fiction is also hinted at in our dream life. In our dreams we find ourselves confronted with a reality that we ignore during our waking life. There we can find the fears and anxieties that we pretend we are immune to, the weaknesses that do not fit into the image we have of ourselves.

The *Miami Vice* episode in question is called "Mirror Image," a title that directly brings to mind the mirror phase: that point in our development when we begin to gain a sense of selfhood described in the first chapter. Not only does this point in our development bring us under the influence of separation and alienation (Original Sin, the Law, and Idolatry), but there is also a moment of fundamental misrecognition in which we begin to take on a foreign notion of ourselves.

We cannot come to self-awareness without giving that awareness some content, any more than we can "see" nothing. We can, of course, have the capacity to see, just as we can have the capacity for self-awareness. But just as actually seeing means that we perceive something, so self-consciousness means being conscious *of* something. That which we are conscious of in ourselves is called the ego. This ego is the image we have of ourselves, the image that we present on a daily basis through work, recreation, and social media.

Theologically speaking, we may call this affirmation of the story we tell ourselves about ourselves a form of Unbelief, for it is the holding of a belief that we don't really believe, a belief that hides the reality that what we really believe is generally not reflected in the image we have of ourselves. We see this expressed beautifully in the parable of a king who returned to his home one day to find a beggar at his gates. Upon seeing this man in rags, the king ran into the palace and summoned one of his servants, saying, "There is a beggar outside; throw him out immediately. Do you not know that I am too kind and compassionate a man to look upon such suffering?"

Is this not the logic we see play out in our own lives on a daily basis? "Do not show me the suffering that takes place in the dairy industry, for I love animals so much that

I cannot bear to see such pain" or "Do not tell me where this shirt was made because I love children too much to hear of their horrific abuse in sweatshops." Here our "beliefs" are nothing more than a form of Unbelief—they are the story we tell ourselves about ourselves in order to avoid the truth. It is Unbelief, because it is fully affirmed as what we believe, while being that which covers over what we actually do believe (evidenced in what we do).

We can see how we hide behind our own image cleverly exposed in a supposedly true story about one of the greatest theologians of the twentieth century who, at the very height of his fame, was invited to participate in a high-society masked orgy. These events were attended by well-known individuals, so everyone who participated was keen to keep their identity a secret. As such, the only thing that people wore was an operatic mask to cover their face.

The great theologian accepted the invitation and arrived at the house on the given night. When he entered the vast room where the orgy was to take place, he was confronted by the sight of dozens of guests who were naked except for the facial covering that hid their identity.

When the host saw this theologian enter the room he was aghast, for he was wearing nothing, not even a face covering. The host ran up to him and pulled him to one side, saying, "This is an anonymous event. What are you doing without a mask?"

To which he replied calmly, "Why, my dear friend, what you see *is* my mask."

Our real beliefs are generally not to be found at the level of ego; rather they are more like the operating system of a computer, they are the heart of the machine that causes it to act in certain ways.

> Our real beliefs are generally not to be found at the level of ego.

Protect Me from What I Know

Before we are born, our parents have a whole host of dreams, hopes, and expectations for us. These might be positive or negative depending upon the situation, but when we are born, these dreams, hopes, and expectations are communicated to us in a whole host of ways. Before we have a sense of our own individuality, we are being called by a particular name and being immersed in a particular story about ourselves—"You are a beautiful girl," "You are such a strong little man," "You are so clever," "You are good," "You are very bad," and the like. As we start to gain a sense of self, we identify with this story that is being told to us about us. When we cry, our parents may say, "You are so brave," or when we have trouble with a basic puzzle, we might be encouraged with the words, "You are such a clever child," while the truth is precisely the opposite: after all, the child is not particularly brave if he is crying or clever if she is having trouble with the puzzle.

One of the reasons we identify so readily with these stories is that they help to cover over the reality of our weakness and helplessness. These stories give us a way of understanding who we are, where we came from, and where we are going. They give us a sense of mastery and importance that belies the truth of our weakness.

If we are called a little prince or a beautiful princess, we readily identify with these images and play into them, as they offer us a fantasy of wholeness and power that obscures the truth that we are incomplete and reliant on others for our ongoing existence. In this way these stories, vital as they are, enable us to hide the truth of our human condition. They help us to feel in control when the reality is that we are largely helpless and weak. The narrative we are given attempts to cover over and mask our actual state. When these stories show signs of structural weakness, we often engage in various tactics in order to cover over the cracks. This is captured cleverly in the following story:

There was once a man who had been shipwrecked on an uninhabited desert island. There he lived alone for ten years before finally being rescued by a passing aircraft. Before leaving the island, one of the rescuers asked if they could see where the man had lived during his time on the island, and so he brought the small group to a clearing where there were three buildings.

Pointing to the first he said, "This was my home; I built it when I first moved here all those years ago."

"What about the building beside it?" asked one of the rescuers.

"Oh, that is where I would worship every week," he replied.

"And the building beside that?"

"Don't bring that up," replied the man in an agitated tone. "That is where I used to worship."

This story exposes and plays with the fact that we are riven with internal conflicts, conflicts that we attempt to avoid by projecting them out. In the above story, the man is unable to maintain the illusion of being right by projecting his inner conflict onto a clash with someone else, so he has to present it in terms of a clash between his present self and past self. The parable thus confronts us with the lengths to which we will go to maintain a narrative of mastery and avoid feeling the anxiety that comes from a sense of unknowing and internal flux. These stories that we grasp onto help us construct an image of ourselves that acts as an anchor; however, in so doing they obscure the truth that we are cast adrift and undone, a truth we attempt to avoid at all costs.

You Are a Haunted House

The way that these stories cover over our brokenness is beautifully hinted at in the movie *Ghost Town*, directed by

David Koepp. On the surface the film operates with much the same structure we see in other films dealing with ghosts. The phantoms are stuck in our world and the protagonist is charged with attempting to work out why they have not passed on to the other side. However, while most stories work with the idea that ghosts are here because they cannot let go of the world, *Ghost Town* presents us with a much more interesting premise. Near the end we discover that the ghosts walk among us not because they have unfinished business with us, but because we have unfinished business with them. It is not that they remain overly attached to our world, but that we remain overly attached to them, refusing to let them go.

In a similar way, there is a deep sense in which we are all ghost towns. We are all haunted by the memory of those we love, those with whom we feel we have unfinished business. While they may no longer be with us, a faint aroma of their presence remains, a presence that haunts us until we make our peace with them and let them go. The problem, however, is that we tend to spend a great deal of energy in attempting to avoid this truth. We construct an image of ourselves that seeks to shield us from a confrontation with our ghosts. Hence we often encounter them only late at night, in the corridors of our dreams.

Just like in *Ghost Town*, we often need someone who is sensitive to these ghosts, someone who can help to bring them to our attention and encourage us to work through why they are there. For the story we have of ourselves is one that often blinds us to these ghosts and dulls our senses to their presence. Our self-image is one that attempts to retain a sense of mastery and togetherness that these ghosts challenge. Yet no matter how hard we try to avoid them, they remain, making their presence felt in subtle but significant ways. Hence the difficulty many of us have with taking time in silent contemplation. When we stop what we are doing and attempt to become still, we discover that there are fears and anxieties within us that clutter up our world. Thus the popular wisdom that we must become silent in order to work things through in our lives covers over a deeper reality—namely, that silent meditation is all but impossible for us because we have so much to work through. In light of this, it might be better to say that the ability to be truly silent with yourself is not the path to peace but a sign that you have found it.

We all have mythologies that we have constructed and adapted from infancy—we cannot exist without them. They are a vital part of our development, even though some can be deeply destructive (when, for instance, we are told that we are unwanted, bad, or good for nothing). Mythologies are overarching stories that tell us why we are here, where we are going, and what we are supposed to do. The problem arises when we fully identify with these mythologies, viewing them as a complete and accurate description of who we are and how the world works—in other words, when it becomes a mask that covers the truth of our anxiety and unknowing.

Instead of facing up to the reality that we are fragile human beings who are faced with mystery and suffering, these narratives help us prop up the fantasy that we are in control of our destinies and are masters of our actions. These fantasies often get challenged only when we go through a tragic life event. At times of extreme flux, the things we may have placed our identity in (work, family life, fitness) are stripped away and the truth is momentarily revealed.

These myths that give us a sense of place and mastery continue to grow and develop as we do. Not only are we given personal stories when we are infants (you are good, strong, brave, etc.), we are given larger political, cultural, and religious stories (you are Christian, Buddhist, capitalist, Marxist, etc.). These larger mythologies operate in the same way as the more personal ones. Such cultural, political, and religious narratives give us a sense of place and purpose. They tell us who we are, why we are here, and what the meaning of our lives is. These stories help us work out who our potential friends might be, whom we should be wary of, and who our enemies are. They inform us about what is civilized and uncivilized, what is right and wrong, what is good and bad, what is significant and insignificant.

> **Instead of facing up to the reality that we are fragile human beings, these narratives help us prop up the fantasy that we are in control of our destiny.**

Even if we rebel against these stories, they still exert their control over us, for that which we oppose is that which we end up defining ourselves against.

We naturally embrace these mythologies that predate our advent into the world and seem likely to continue long after we have passed away. Their stability and power are deeply seductive. By embracing these cultural, political, and religious narratives and by identifying so directly with them, we gain a sense of knowing the truth, of having a God's eye perspective on the world.

These narratives offer us a sense of mastery, a way of understanding things that might otherwise appear foreign, peculiar, and frightening. When we are faced with pain, these narratives offer us a way of understanding it and giving it significance. They act as a type of compass that helps us navigate our world.

Whitewashed Tombs

Within the Christian scriptures we read of Jesus coming into contact with a group of religious leaders who affirm a set of beliefs that cover over the truth of their inner lives. When confronted with this Unbelief, Jesus says, "Woe to you, teachers of the law and Pharisees, you hypocrites! You are like whitewashed tombs, which look beautiful on the outside but on the inside are full of dead men's bones and everything unclean. In the same way, on the outside you appear to people as righteous but on the inside you are full of hypocrisy and wickedness." (Matthew 23:27–28)

Jesus is here pointing out the gulf that exists between how these teachers present themselves and what is buried in their hearts. These teachers have an image of being upright, good, and moral, but Jesus is saying that this image covers over what lies inside.

It is tempting to think that Jesus is chastising these leaders because of their inner darkness, but this doesn't really make sense in relation to the wider trajectory of the Gospels, which accepts people in their brokenness. The issue at hand is the disparity between the image they present (an image that they no doubt affirm) and the reality. They are covering over what lies within by offering a false image, much like an alcoholic who might deny the truth of his addiction, even to himself.

We can contrast this condemnation with the parable of the tax collector who acknowledges his darkness and is praised. The Pharisees have not found a way of expressing their darkness, and so it festers in the unconscious as an unacknowledged reality. It is only as we admit to our captivity to Unbelief that we can begin to confront what we truly believe in our hearts.

While these religious teachers are not being honest about the truth of their beliefs, it would be wrong to think that Jesus is angry because they are somehow lying to others. It is much more likely that the religious leaders are actually lying, first and foremost, to themselves. It is hard for us to think of ourselves as broken, so we deny it even though it is obviously true.

Again, this can be compared to an alcoholic who denies the reality of his addiction; for more often than not the one he is deceiving is himself. He keeps telling himself that he could give up at any time, that he is not really drinking that much, and that people are overreacting.

> It is hard for us to think of ourselves as bad or broken, so we deny these things even though they are obviously true.

The point is that he is denying to himself what is plainly obvious; he is dimly aware of the truth but is repressing it. *He is refusing to know what he knows.*

The religious leaders Jesus is addressing would no doubt feel misunderstood and indignant about his accusations. For their ego (their image of themselves) is not simply a cover to help them maintain a positive image in front of others; more fundamentally, it provides a way for them to maintain a positive image before themselves.

The problem that Jesus is pointing out is not the gulf that lies between what these religious teachers say and what they think, but the gulf that exists between what these religious teachers pretend to be and what they are.

The concept of the heart that is referred to in the biblical text is not equivalent to the mind; rather, it is closer to the modern concept of the unconscious. It represents the often unacknowledged truth of who we are, a truth that we hide from our own consciousness. It is, however, a truth that makes itself known in a vast array of ways, such as through aggressive behavior, self-hatred, dislike of others, overeating, overworking, drug abuse, etc.

We all are tempted to fall into the same trap as these religious teachers whom Jesus chastised; we want to hold to the image we have of ourselves and our world because it is a fiction that gives us a sense of place, purpose, and perspective. Our various foundational beliefs about the world, God, and ourselves act like a shield protecting us from a full confrontation with what we really believe.

I Need Your Eyes to Help Me See

Another danger with affirming our various religious, political, and cultural narratives as reflections of the truth is that when we encounter people with different founding stories, they strike us as perverse, monstrous, and threatening. This reality is generally played down, disavowed, or left unspoken by communities, but it often rises to the surface when one community comes into close proximity with another. At these times the opposing worldviews clash and each side is experienced as a threat by the other. The way that we initially encounter the other is captured in the following story.

One evening a young man returning home after a long and tiring day at work gets a call from his concerned wife.

"Dear, be careful on the way home, as I just heard on the radio that some crazy guy has been spotted going full speed the wrong way up the freeway."

"Sorry, love," he shouts back, "can't talk right now. There isn't just one nutter, *there are thousands of them*!!!"

One of the interesting things to note about this little anecdote is the way that the husband does not even entertain the possibility that he might be going the wrong way. Instead he takes it for granted that he is right. This is not a belief he is conscious of; rather all his conscious thoughts are filtered through this belief.

When we encounter a worldview different from our own, there are four common responses.

The first involves engaging in a form of *consumption*, by which we attempt to integrate the other into our social body, much like eating an animal makes it a part of our physical body. Here the other is made into a version of ourselves, just as the Borg in the Star Trek universe integrate any species they find into their singular collective. The Borg consume other species in order to strengthen, enhance, and advance their own collective. In this way the Borg are inherently a conservative force in that they attempt to conserve their own structure instead of opening it up to genuine transformation by an encounter with the outside.

By attempting to consume the other, we strive to

render them into our like-
ness, a process that involves
an apologetic strategy in
which we attempt to per-
suade them that they should
believe and practice in a
particular way.

> **By attempting to
> consume the other, we
> strive to render them
> into our likeness.**

The second approach is intimately connected with the
first and can be described as the act of *vomiting* the other
out. This means that anything within our social body that
cannot be properly integrated is pushed out. It is a process
of exclusion whereby we condemn and reject the other
who cannot be consumed by us. They are thus viewed as
an enemy that must be excluded from our institutions, an
enemy whom we must insulate ourselves from to avoid
contamination.

The third approach is where an individual or community responds to someone different from themselves
via *toleration*. In this approach, there is an attempt to
accept the other, even though they seem strange to us.
We continue to work alongside them, buy from the
same shops, and even relate to them in areas of common
interest. Toleration in the West is premised upon the
existence of a public square in which our various differences remain hidden. People can believe and practice a
variety of strange and obscure things behind closed doors
as long as it isn't visible in public places. The toleration
is thus exposed as a form of accepting the presence of the
other so long as their otherness is not directly expressed.

The fourth common response to someone who is different from us is that of a dialogue aimed at finding *agreement*. At its most simplistic, it is the idea that beneath all our little differences, we're really pretty much the same. We may give different names to things, but we are broadly worshipping the same God or upholding the same values. While there are some small moral differences, we operate within the same ethical framework.

Amidst their obvious differences, each of these responses to the other (consumption, vomiting, toleration, and agreement) share something significant in common: in each of them we stand over the other.

In all four we judge the outsider from our position. In the first three, I am right and the other is wrong, while in the fourth we are both largely right. In other words, when I approach the other, I approach them from a higher position, deciding whether to agree or disagree with them in relation to my already established beliefs and practices. We are thus looking down upon their tradition, even when we affirm it—for we are affirming it only insofar as it aligns with our own.

There is, however, a different way of approaching the other. This different approach involves placing ourselves beneath them in the sense of allowing their views to challenge and unsettle our own.

One of the ways that this can be done is through a form of *literalistic listening*. I use this term to differentiate it from the type of listening we do on a daily basis, where we filter what a person is saying through our own experiences. This normal kind of listening leads us to miss what the other is saying unless it makes sense within our current value system, beliefs, and practices.

I remember this happening to me when I talked to a friend who was considering a separation from his partner. During the conversation he began sharing about the fear he had about damaging his children. At one point he said, "You know, my parents went through a similar thing and it really tore us apart." I signaled my understanding, internally agreeing that separation can be very difficult for children. It was only the next day that I remembered that my friend's parents were still together. When I pointed this out to him, he explained to me that this was the problem. I had assumed that his parents had split up because of my underlying view that this is the only way that he and his siblings could have been damaged, but the truth was that they had been damaged because his parents had stayed together in an unhappy marriage.

I had filtered his words through my own lens and instead of paying attention to what he was saying, I simply made his words fit with my own underlying assumptions. In this way I was able to domesticate his words rather than letting them have an impact on and destabilize me.

> **Instead of paying attention to what he was saying, I simply made his words fit with my own underlying assumptions.**

It is, of course, impossible not to hear things from

one's own position, but it is possible to listen in a sensitive and careful way that has the power to unsettle our preconceived ideas. This means that one pays attention to what the other says, allowing the words and phrases to place our own assumptions into question.

We do not do this very often because we spend most of our time with people who share views of the world that are similar to our own. But when we sensitize ourselves to the other's discourse, listening for points of dispute, the other's discourse can rupture our own presuppositions and cause us to reflect upon the things we would otherwise take for granted.

In literalistic listening we take careful note of everything the other says from their position instead of quickly interpreting it in relation to our own position. Instead of a monologue shared by two people, it can then become a genuine dialogue in the sense of two different positions meeting in such a way as to generate a potentially transformative conversation for both parties.

Instead of approaching those with different beliefs and practices from a position of strength—in which we simply engage in the act of agreement or disagreement (which means comparing the other in relation to our own pre-established horizon)—literalistic listening asks us to approach from a position of weakness. It means that we don't simply look at the other through our own eyes, but we attempt to look at ourselves through the eyes of the other.

The result is that, instead of seeing the other as strange and alien, we actually begin to encounter ourselves as strange and alien; we begin to glimpse how the things that we take to be eternally true are actually constructs with a history. Instead of agreeing or disagreeing with the other, we ask, "What do I look like to you?" In doing this we do not simply filter what they say through our lens but are confronted by the reality of our lens.

The Church as the Support of Unbelief

Unfortunately, the church today does not help to expose the contingency of our various mythologies but joins with other institutions in putting a mythology forth as the truth. Indeed, the church often turns out to be the most extreme agent of this myth-making: it doesn't simply offer a narrative that tells us who we are, why we are here, and where we are going, but it tells people that this narrative has been directly delivered by the divine. The church thus takes the crown among all groups that claim insight into the nature of existence.

This can help us understand why Marx made the claim that the beginning of all critique is the critique of religion.* For religion not only mirrors

> Religion not only mirrors the problem that enslaves us but does so in an exaggerated and extreme way.

---

*Karl Marx, *Early Writings*, trans. Rodney Livingstone and Gregor Benton (New York: Vintage Books, 1975), p. 243.

71

the problem that enslaves us but does so in an exaggerated and extreme way.

While other institutions might claim to offer a product that will make us whole and a story that will inform us of who we are, they generally do not claim that their Idol is God and their narrative God-given.

Sadly, then, the church today does not offer an alternative to the Idolatry and Unbelief that weigh us down, but instead blesses them and gives them divine justification. The question that faces us, then, is how Christianity, in its most radical and subversive form, critiques the church and offers real freedom.

Part Two

THE NEW CREATION

CHAPTER 4

Be Part of the Problem,
Not the Solution

The Zombie Apocalypse
Has Already Happened

One of the defining aspects of being human is an obsessive drive for the Idol, a drive that is both part of our humanity and yet undermines it. Other animals lack this drive—they do not show an obsessive attachment to a goal beyond the satisfaction of basic needs. Interestingly it is in the animal kingdom, not the human world, that we see the ethical system of utilitarianism lived out consistently. It is there that we find the perfect expression of J. S. Mill's ethical vision, one in which actions are calculated in relation to the amount of pleasure they give or pain they avoid.

When it comes to human beings, however, it is evident that we are infused with a drive that places this rational calculation into question, a compulsion that arises from the experience of Original Sin in direct confrontation with the Law.

It is the reality of this drive that helps us understand the genesis of zombie mythology, for zombies express this pure drive completely divorced from any social constraints or self-interested pursuit of pleasure. In this way, the zombie will do anything in its desire for human flesh, even if it involves its own ultimate destruction. The zombie then expresses pure human drive without the social and psychological constraints that keep it in check. The undead obsessively pursue something beyond the mere satisfaction of a need.

> The zombie will do anything in its desire for human flesh, even if it involves its own ultimate destruction.

Zombies reflect an aspect of our own nature back to us in a pure and undiluted form. They express what is most uniquely human about us—that which is absent from other animals. But, in doing so, the undead also express that part of our being that makes us feel inhuman, that part that places us into direct conflict with ourselves and those around us.

So then, the zombie is not some alien creature that uses the empty shell of human beings in order to live, but instead is the overwhelming dominance of one aspect of our being—a drive—existing beyond the death of everything else.

When we watch a zombie film, there is a very real sense in which we are being directly confronted with an image of what it is that makes us what we are. In this way the zombie apocalypse isn't coming; it is already here. It happened at the very birth of the human race. The zombie is within us.

This is one of the insights found in the *Walking Dead* comic. What we find here is not the usual mythology that describes a (false) qualitative gap between human and zombie (if we are bitten, then "we" die and the empty shell of our body is reanimated as a zombie). Instead we discover that the human race is already zombies in waiting. We do not become zombies when we are bitten by one; rather, we emerge as zombies whenever we die. The virus is thus already a part of us rather than being some foreign agent. It simply becomes manifest when everything else in us dies. The drive reanimates our bodies and now finds full expression without constraint.

Give Me Freedom from the Pursuit of My Satisfaction

With this in mind we can begin to understand one of the limits of a political system that operates with the idea of people acting in their own self-interest.

In the pragmatic work of politics in the West, we might say that the goal is to engage in the difficult task of working out and implementing systems that offer people the freedom to pursue their highest ambitions. In practice this involves many difficult and complex debates concerning such things as the role of government and the rights of groups relative to the rights of individuals, as well as a host of practical constraints, cultural realities, and changing circumstances. All of which combine to make the work demanding and difficult.

It is commonly believed that society functions best when its population is able to pursue what it desires, a pursuit that is constrained in only minimal ways (protecting others, making sure that contracts are honored, etc.). The idea is that a happy society is one in which we have the ability—hypothetically at least—to gain the fame, money, relationship, creative venture, lover, or family life that we seek. If our dreams are impossible to achieve in actuality, then we are effectively living in a type of oppressive, totalitarian regime that leads to a discontented, depressed, and angry population.

One of the claims that is often made about a system that enables people to pursue their own happiness is that the self-interested nature of human beings is harnessed and used to benefit everyone. In contrast to a system that might demand that we think of others before ourselves, it is said, there is something profoundly natural about our selfishness.

People who advocate self-interested systems are often

not justifying them as moral. Their point is simply that any system that does not take people's selfishness seriously is naïve and utopian. "Perhaps, if there is a heaven," they say, "we will find a different way for people to interact. But here we must create systems that can harness the power of people pursuing their own passions for the good of all."

The underlying belief is that a political system that is built upon people's rational pursuit of their own pleasure reflects human beings' natural tendencies and thus is not so much an ideological system as a reflection of nature.

One of the blind spots with such a reading, however, is the way that those people who are driven to achieve great things are often very selfless individuals, albeit a selflessness that resembles what we witness in zombie movies. A zombie, as we have already mentioned, will seek to consume flesh even when its very existence is at stake. It is driven to achieve a goal beyond any normal consideration of cost/benefit analysis and will pursue it to its own demise. There are any number of successful investors, for example, who if they were truly selfish, would stop what they were doing at a certain point instead of pursuing more at the expense of their health, relationships, and mental stability.

Instead of retiring with a nice sum of money, many successful businesspeople continue on with a seemingly insatiable appetite, even though they are aware of the negative effect it has on their loved ones and their own bodies.

If such a person were to sit down and do an objective analysis of his drive in a dispassionate, utilitarian manner, he would likely see that his obsession is not enhancing his life but actually destroying it. Indeed, people who are driven to pursue something like wealth or fame are often painfully aware of this reality. At certain points they will even, over a drink, confess that their desire is not liberating but oppressive and that they would like to be free of it so that they could more fully enjoy the relationships, possessions, and lifestyle they already have. What we see here is a concrete example of how the freedom to pursue our highest ambitions is often not experienced as a freedom from an oppressive system but is itself felt to be oppressive.

> The freedom to pursue our highest ambitions is often not experienced as a freedom from an oppressive system but is itself felt to be oppressive.

Political freedom often leads to a society with greater material wealth and better opportunities for the population, which are to be highly valued. But there is another, more radical form of freedom hinted at in the Gospels—not the freedom to pursue what we believe will satisfy us, but the freedom *from* the pursuit of what we believe will satisfy us.

Unless we also have freedom from the pursuit of what we believe will satisfy us, political freedom can be experienced as one of the most psychologically powerful forms of oppression. Freedom from the pursuit of satisfaction should, however, be distinguished from a system that explicitly prevents us from pursuing what we believe will satisfy us, for the latter is something that is imposed upon us. A system that prevents us from pursuing the things we believe will satisfy acts as the Law, i.e., as that which prohibits something, thus making it even more desirable.

There is something, however, that a seemingly free system does offer, despite its best efforts to the contrary: *internal protest*.

Because totalitarian systems place an external constraint on the population, it encourages inner protest. We may not be allowed to get what we think we truly want, but we can hate that fact and blame the government for it.

The philosopher Slavoj Žižek compares this to what we see in a family where a child is forced by her parents to go and visit a relative whom she doesn't really like. The child is not given a choice, but she can at least resist internally. Thus she goes to see the relative while imagining the freedom she might have if she were older and didn't have to.

In contrast, the type of oppression that comes from our ability to pursue what we want does not allow us to maintain this minimal inner protest. For now no external constraint is being imposed. The message a person gets from such a society is that there are no limits—go on, pursue whatever you like. The problem is that now we have no one to blame for our unhappiness. We cannot say to ourselves, "I would be happy if only this government was overthrown" or "I could have what I want if the corporations were not controlling everything." We are free to pursue what we want; in fact, we are actively encouraged to do so everywhere we turn.

Popular films, music, and magazines all seem to be telling us the same thing: "Go for it." Only when we are confronted with this command to enjoy do we discover the voice that tells us "Just do it" is actually more insidiously oppressive than the voice that says "You can't do it." For the latter is an external constraint that allows us to maintain a small inner protest, while the former gets under our skin. The former voice implicitly tells us that we can't blame anyone but ourselves for our enduring lack of fulfillment.

This is why Žižek playfully points out that the modern parent who tells her child he doesn't need to visit Granny but that she really wants to see him and it will be lots of fun to go can be more oppressive than just forcing the child into the car. For the child's freedom to choose is a farce (he will have to go regardless), and not only does he have to go, but it is being asked of him that he *want* to go, to like what he doesn't actually like. The child thus engages in an activity he "wants" to do (internalizing the message that it will be fun), while feeling a certain oppression.

It is this logic that Mother Teresa put her finger on when she saw all the depression and sadness of the developed world, something that she did not experience to the same degree in Calcutta. For her it was more insidious because blatant poverty could be seen and addressed, but this psychological poverty was experienced from within as a type of demon dwelling beneath the surface of our skin. It is a poverty that has found a way to hide in the most unlikely of places: in wealth itself.

> **This psychological poverty was experienced from within as a type of demon dwelling beneath the surface of our skin.**

It was an insidious form of slavery that wore the mask of freedom.

Giving Up Fulfillment to Find Peace

The problem, for most of us, is not that there is a lack of things we should be able to get enjoyment from, but that we are unable to actually enjoy these things. The Idol robs us of the type of pleasure that we could have if only we were able to free ourselves from the false promise that something would render us complete. But in order to get to this more grounded and deep happiness, we must first take a hammer to the Idol. It is only as we lay down the promise of fullness proclaimed by this false god and begin to embrace the world that we can discover a true joy.

We see this beautifully expressed in the film *WALL-E*. The story revolves around the premise that humans have left earth because pollution resulting from our insatiable desire to consume has made it uninhabitable. Humans have opted to temporarily live in a huge spaceship called *Axiom* until the earth is habitable again. They originally intended to leave for five years, but when the film begins, they are in their seven hundredth year. Before leaving earth, the humans left an army of robots charged with the task of cleaning up the mess. But over the years, all but one of these robots have broken down.

The idea of humans leaving earth and going to live in the heavens offers a direct parallel of the notion of heaven found in the popular imagination. The spacecraft is a place where all one's needs are met, a place where there is no pain or suffering, tension or conflict, and no one has a job to do (except the captain, whose role is largely a symbolic one). It is a place of perpetual peace, harmony, and relaxation. While we can presume that people still grow old and die, the film does not show any of this.

However, it turns out that this "heavenly" existence is actually a type of mundane, melancholic hell. No one walks anymore (they all use hovercrafts to move), everyone is overweight, and humanity is portrayed, via a scene in which we see portraits of different captains, as slowly devolving.

In contrast to films like *Equilibrium*, this dystopia was not forced on people—human beings chose it freely; it is what they want, or at least what they think they want.

They do not hate it any more than they love it; they have entered into a type of stasis not unlike a cryogenic state, in which they are not really dead and yet not fully alive.

Once the film has shown us how this first ("heavenly") attempt at salvation and fulfillment has failed, it charts humanity's return to earth. As humans slowly turn from their reliance on technology and desire for instant gratification, they begin to experience joy and wonder again.

This is not, however, a naïve vision in which the director paints rural life as one of true peace and tranquility. This is to miss the point—their heavenly existence *did* offer peace and tranquility in a direct, unmediated way (not some false version of these) and was, for this very reason, the true enemy of existence. Instead, by forsaking this direct, horrifying engagement with peace and tranquility and living up to the fact that life involves a host of tensions and difficulties, the film expresses how a more substantive life can be rediscovered.

In this we see a glimpse of the idea that heaven, in the popular sense, would be a type of living death, but that truly embracing the fragility and tensions of life, supremely difficult as this is, brings with it the possibility of true joy.

By returning to the very thing that they thought was the obstacle to their fulfillment, they indirectly find it.

> **Truly embracing the fragility and tensions of life, supremely difficult as this is, brings with it the possibility of true joy.**

This can remind us of what Dietrich Bonhoeffer was thinking when he wrote,

> This is what I mean by worldliness—taking life in one's stride, with all its duties and problems, its successes and failures, its experiences and helplessness. It is in such a life that we throw ourselves into the arms of God and participate in his sufferings in the world and watch with Christ in Gethsemane. That is faith, that is metonoia and that is what makes a man and a Christian.*

In this way we learn that heaven is discovered only when we renounce it and put ourselves to the task of embracing our world.

Here we start to approach what can be called the Good News of Christianity: *You can't be fulfilled; you can't be made whole; you can't find satisfaction.*

> You can't be fulfilled; you can't be made whole; you can't find satisfaction.

At first this can sound like anything but good news; however, once we are freed from the oppression of the Idol, we find that embracing and loving life—with all its difficulties—offers a much deeper and richer form of joy. The Good News is not simply a

---

*John de Gruchy, ed., *Selected Writings of Dietrich Bonhoeffer* (London: Collins, 1987), p. 294.

confrontation with the reality that total fulfillment and certainty are not possible, but rather is found in the joyful embrace of this insight. An embrace that robs the reality of its oppressive sting.

The advocates of Christianity often present Christ as the solution to the problem posed by the universal sense of separation and alienation lurking at the core of our being.

But Christianity, at its most radical, is not the solution to the problem posed by separation and alienation. It places this entire framework into question. Christianity does not offer a salvation that operates within this frame, but instead opens up the possibility of a salvation from this frame.

Christ and Value

In order to understand how the Gospels hint at a freedom from this slavery to the Idol, we must begin by exploring the meaning of the idea that Christ is without sin. From the line of thought that we have been developing, this means that Christ is experienced as one who lacks the lack. In other words, as one without a sense of separation at the very core of his being and thus without any attachment to some Idol that would falsely promise to make him whole.

The Christian tradition goes on to claim that Christ took on sin on the Cross. In order to understand the meaning of this claim, we can use the example of money. Money itself has no value but represents all value. Of course the money we use on a daily basis has some very tiny value because it is made from materials that can be bought and sold (paper, copper, etc.). But money in its pure abstraction has no value whatsoever. It is what we use to stand in for value, thus enabling the smooth exchange of goods and services. The best way to understand this is to think of how money functions in the stock market. Money there exists in purely numeric form; it has no materiality and is thus without any value while representing pure value.

Just as money has no value and yet comes to represent all value, the early church presented Christ on the Cross as being without sin and yet representing all sin. It is therefore claimed that he lacked the foundational separation constitutive of human beings (the gap that renders them inhuman), yet he took on that gap and felt it in its most acute form.

This is the radical message of the Cross, not that a man is tortured and killed, but that one who is without the lack experienced the incision that marks us all: fully and completely feeling that cut in our being that prevents us from being at one with ourselves.

> The radical message of the Cross is not that a man is tortured and killed, but that one who is without the lack experienced the incision that marks us all.

It is this that we bear witness to in the cry "My God, my God, why have you forsaken me?" For in this cry we witness Christ experience that profound sense of separation and alienation that marks all human beings.

Before moving on, it is important to note a second way that Christ's relation to sin can be compared to money. For Christ is said to take on our debt, and money is the concrete manifestation of debt. The entire monetary system came about as a way of measuring and recording the debt that people felt within communities. It is popular for people to think that primitive societies engaged in a form of bartering in which two people would exchange goods. However, this is not quite the case for it has been found that ancient societies operated with a system more like what we see play out today around the etiquette of dinner invitations. Let us imagine that a couple has been invited to someone's house for the gift of a meal. They do not immediately seek to repay the kindness (for example, to try and pay for the meal would be offensive and embarrassing). Instead they leave with a sense of indebtedness that results in them later inviting the original hosts for a dinner at their place. The exchange does not take place at the same time (something that would relieve the sense of debt), but rather occurs over time. While on the surface, such exchanges are experienced as gifts, if the reciprocity does not happen, socially awkward situations arise. The way in which indebtedness flows between friends helps to solidify and deepen social relations.

In the same way, this type of free flow of debt expresses some of the earliest ways in which societies exchanged goods and ensured stronger social bonds. Take the example of someone who owns a number of sheep who is approached by his neighbor who owns chickens. The neighbor may need a sheep but that doesn't mean that the sheep's owner needs chickens. Instead of a direct barter taking place, the owner of the sheep gives it to his neighbor without a demand for any immediate return. However, at a later date, when he might need chickens, the neighbor, who feels indebted, will offer him some. In this way the sense of debt is relieved. Money was later brought in as a means of measuring and recording this complex system of debt, and it radically changed the original system of social relations.

The important thing to realize about debt, then, is that it is a form of void, a nothing. Debt is a type of lack and money stands in to represent it, just as Original Sin is a type of lack and Christ offers us a direct manifestation of this loss on the Cross.

The Nothing Is Revealed to Be Nothing

The meaning of Christ being without sin and yet taking sin onto himself is deceptively simple. It means that Christ is understood to experience the horror of separation and alienation from the Idol that actually creates the void. He feels Original Sin, the Law, and the birth of Idolatry; but because he is not enslaved by them, we witness their abolition in the text.

In this way we not only see the power of separation and alienation from the Idol (which we see in Christ's cry of dereliction), but also the truth that the entire matrix of Original Sin, the Law, and Idolatry is a fiction.

This second part of the Crucifixion is seen when we read of the Temple curtain in Jerusalem being torn from top to bottom (Matthew 27:51). This curtain was a thick veil that was believed to separate the people from God. The temple was constructed in such a way that the people would constantly be aware of their separation and alienation from God. The people could enter the temple but not the Holy of Holies, which lay just beyond the curtain (that can be said to represent the law). Only the high priest could enter and only once a year in a highly orchestrated way.

When the temple curtain is ripped apart, the truth of the whole separation/alienation system is seen for what it is, for we discover something utterly shocking: *there is nothing behind the curtain*. What Original Sin and the Law caused us to think we are separated from is a fiction; with the destruction of the Law, the Idol is abolished.

This is not to say that the Jewish faith operates with a lie that is revealed in Christianity. The reality is more interesting than this.

First, the idea that what we feel separated from is fiction can be found within the Jewish faith itself. There are key elements of the Hebrew scriptures that bear witness to what we see born out on the Cross. I will give two quick examples. The first is in the book of Ecclesiastes, in which the teacher continually reminds us that everything is meaningless. This is not the lesson of the book, but the reality that we must experience in order to touch upon its message—which is that in the midst of the belief that life has no meaning (the loss of the Idol), life can still be experienced as meaningful in the embrace and affirmation of existence itself: through eating, drinking, and being joyful in our life as it is. Here there is a subversive message that tells us that the loss of "God" (the religious Idol), while traumatic, can open up to a new experience of God dwelling in the midst, something that is affirmed in the very act of embracing life.

> The loss of "God" (the religious Idol), while traumatic, can open up to a new experience of God dwelling in the midst, something that is affirmed in the very act of embracing life.

The second example is the Jewish prohibition against making graven images of the divine. The perverse reading of this prohibition is one that sees it as actually generating what it explicitly condemns. This is like someone asking a person not to imagine something in order to make them imagine it. But this is not how the prohibition functions within the Jewish tradition. Historically speaking, this prohibition has been expressed in a very grounded way that emphasizes the idea of God being affirmed in community and tradition.

In this way we can see how the Jewish faith already holds what is revealed on the Cross; what we see in Christianity is this truth being brought wholly to the surface, a truth that is quickly buried again in the theological apologetics of the actually existing church, which has proved unable to bear witness to the true scandal of faith.

The Sacrifice of Sacrifice Itself

So how are we to approach the sacrifice of Christ on the Cross? There are a variety of ways in which Christ's death has been understood; however, we can largely place them into two camps. The first could be called the conservative readings, and it goes something like this: We are separated from God by our misdeeds and deserve death, for God is holy and must punish our wrongdoing. We do not have anything that can free us from this judgment, for blood must be spilt. The solution was that Jesus, one without misdeeds, came to earth and died in our place. His blood paid the price of God's wrath, and so, if we accept the sacrifice of Jesus, our wrongdoing is paid for in full. A slight variation of this atonement theory, which is older, works with the same logic; however, it is not God who needs to be paid in blood but Satan, who has dominion over us. This reading views the sacrifices in the Hebrew scriptures as a foretelling of Christ's sacrifice (the blood of an actual lamb pointing toward the blood of Christ as the Lamb of God); it also sees the tearing of the temple curtain as a sign that Christ is now the "curtain" we must pass through in order to enter the Holy of Holies.

In contrast to these substitution theories, the progressive and liberal parts of the church have often emphasized a different reading that has its roots in the teachings of the early church fathers, called the "moral influence theory." According to this approach, Jesus taught us to embrace a life of love and forgiveness at any cost. He exemplified this message in everything he said and did, including on the Cross. The meaning of the Crucifixion, then, is not that it accomplishes some act that would otherwise keep us apart from God, but that it shows us the way that we ought to live and the cost that such a life might extract.

There is, however, a different approach to understanding the Crucifixion. A third approach sees the Crucifixion neither as the ultimate sacrifice nor as a moral message unrelated to the religious structure of sacrifice, but as the sacrifice of sacrifice itself.

In the conservative reading, Original Sin and the Law are taken seriously, but the Crucifixion is seen as an answer to the problem they pose instead of that which robs them of their sting. In contrast, the liberal reading does not take Original Sin and the Law seriously, but views the Crucifixion as a type of moral tale. To properly understand the experience testified to in the Crucifixion, we must understand it as manifesting an invitation to exist beyond slavery to Idolatry and Unbelief.

The Crucifixion fulfills the sacrificial model in much the same way as love fulfills the Law. For the apostle Paul, love is understood as fulfilling the Law, not by being an überlaw, but by raising us into a different register where we live beyond the prohibition. Instead of being a larger "no," which says that nothing is permissible, love fulfills the law by turning the "no" into a "yes," telling us that, while not everything is beneficial, everything is permissible (1 Corinthians 6:12).

Christ "pays" the debt by forgiving it. On the Cross we witness the day of Jubilee in action, the day of Jubilee was a never-enacted time in ancient Israel when debts were not to be reckoned, but dissipated. In other words, Original Sin and the Law are obliterated and the Idol they create dissolves into thin air.

> **On the Cross, Original Sin and the Law are obliterated and the Idol they create dissolves into thin air.**

Thus, to speak of Christ paying the debt doesn't mean that debt is taken seriously, but that the debt itself is abolished.

To understand how this might look, let us reflect upon the following story:

There was once a very rich Texan who started to look into his ancestral roots. After a little research he discovered that his great-grandfather left Ireland to settle in America and that there was a relative of his called Seamus who still had a small farm in Galway. The next day he flew out to visit Seamus and reconnect with his roots. When he finally found the farm, he knocked on the door and introduced himself.

"Would you like to see the property?" said Seamus to his guest.

"Why, yes."

So Seamus took the large Texan round to the back of the little house and pointed at a tree that stood about fifty feet away.

"See that tree?" he said. "That marks the northern boundary of my land."

Then he pointed at a rusty old tractor in the distance. "That there marks the western border."

"And that," he said, pointing to a broken fence, "marks the eastern border."

"Well," said the Texan with a patronizing smile, "back home, if I got into my car and drove all day north, I still wouldn't reach the border of my land. Indeed, if I drove all day east or west, I wouldn't get to the border of my property."

"Yeah," said Seamus while nodding, "I know how you feel. I used to have a car like that."

While the Texan is obviously trying to show off that he has so much (pretending he has that which brings satisfaction), Seamus does not get caught up in the lie. While he misunderstands what the Texan is both directly saying and indirectly implying, the reason for this misunderstanding is partially due to his being freed from the system of Idolatry. For those caught within the matrix of Original Sin, the Law, and Idolatry are deeply attuned to any discourse that tells us we are incomplete or that another is whole. The only way to completely miss such implications in a person's speech is if you fully acknowledge that we are all broken, that none of us have the Idol, and that we are at peace with that. In short, not getting caught up in the type of false claims reflected in the speech of the Texan hints at the type of freedom testified to in the event of the Crucifixion.

This means that the Crucifixion bears witness to a form of life that is free from our obsessive drive for the Idol, a form of life in which our zombie nature is cured. For to lose the Idol means to be freed from that drive that prevents us from fully embracing our life and taking pleasure in it. It means giving up our desire for ultimate satisfaction and then, in that act, discovering a deeper, more beautiful satisfaction, one that is not constantly deferred but that can be grasped here and now. Not one that promises to make us whole and remove our suffering but one that promises joy in the midst of our brokenness and new life in the very embrace of our pain.

CHAPTER 5

Trash of the World

Crucifixion and the Loss of Meaning

In addition to expressing a form of life that can break us free from the desire to find wholeness and satisfaction, the other freedom that the Crucifixion testifies to is liberation from that second, but deeply intertwined, oppressive system: Unbelief.

We have already explored how Unbelief is formed and the way that so much of the church supports it by offering us yet another grand narrative that tells us why we are here, where we are going, and what we ought to be doing. However, what we find in the event that gave birth to Christianity is something far more powerful than one more master mythology designed to cover over our unknowing and anxiety. For here we do not find yet another system of meaning to place alongside all the others but a type of splinter that disturbs all meaning systems and calls them into question.

In order to understand this we must pay careful attention to the meaning crucifixion had at the time of Jesus. For Roman citizens crucifixion was the most potent sign of someone being rejected by the cultural, political, and religious systems of the day, all of which were seen as divinely established. Those who were crucified were treated as complete outsiders. They were to die naked, alone, and in agony. But the execution meant more than torture and death; it was a sign that the one being killed stood outside of the divinely given order.

> Crucifixion meant more than torture and death; it was a sign that the one being killed stood outside of the divinely given order.

In contrast the Crucifixion of Christ today is seen as a key justification of a cultural, political, and religious matrix, a matrix that Kierkegaard called "Christendom." It is difficult for us today to understand the extent to which this mode of execution signaled the exclusion of the victim from all systems of meaning, because it is so much a part of one for us. The Cross is so integrated into our religious, political, and cultural imagination that its reality as a mode of execution that placed the victim outside of these realms is utterly eclipsed. Instead of being a symbol of standing outside all systems of meaning, the Cross is now integrated into a system of meaning.

Christian Universalism

With this in mind we can begin to approach a properly Christian notion of universalism. In the contemporary church, there are two dominant understandings of the term. First, there is the conservative version, which refers to the idea that the Christian message is for all. Here Christianity is understood as universal inasmuch as its message is not restricted to some particular group, time, or place.

One of the issues that arises as a result of this universalism is how to deal with those who do not accept the message. In contrast to particularist religions (such as Judaism or Islam), which have a place (even if it is an inferior one) for other groups, this type of Christian universalism ends up placing those who do not accept the message into the category of "lost." This effectively places someone on the outside; it is the place of no place, the site of divine curse (interestingly, this location actually mimics the place of Christ on the Cross—the ultimate outsider, cursed by God).

Second, there is a view of universalism that could be broadly described as liberal. This approach sees the effective power of the Christian message as an umbrella that ultimately shelters all. It not only sees the message of Christianity as something that is for everyone but goes on to view its power as touching everyone. The idea of a Christian worldview is still upheld, only unlike the conservative vision, it is believed that everyone will eventually benefit from it.

However, there is a third way of understanding Christian universalism, one that moves us into an utterly different field than these other understandings. Both of the above positions hold to the reality of a concrete Christian identity—in the first those who do not participate in this identity are referred to as "the lost," while in the second, everyone will eventually be grafted in. In this way they are not opposites but rather operate with the same underlying idea. In contrast, the type of universalism we see expressed by the apostle Paul operates on a fundamentally different level by inviting everyone into a community in which everyone exists beyond or outside the operative power of any given identity, including a Christian one. The point for Paul is that our given identities need to be transcended. Whether we are Republican or Democrat, rich or poor, male or female, these various bearers of our identification do not fully contain or constrain us and all too often prevent us from truly experiencing our own humanity. For Paul, the identity of the Christian is found in the very experience of feeling the impotence of all identities.

The Conflict Between Tribes

There are so many divisions in society—divisions between political parties, religious traditions, and social groups. This is perfectly natural, of course. From birth, we experience a preexisting matrix of beliefs and practices that differentiate us from others.

We discover early on that we have been given a mantle, that we are part of a tribe, one with a rich history, deep hopes, and a variety of fears. The world is full of "us" and "them." Some of these divisions have deep histories that span multiple generations, while others are very new. Some are serious and others border on the ridiculous. At their most extreme, these divisions can result in local and global conflicts.

More often than not, the reasons we reject another arise after the actual rejection. We already know that "they" are bad before we have any concrete reasons. This becomes clear when one receives multiple contradictory justifications for disliking a different community. For example, we often hear of racist groups hating immigrants because they believe that the immigrants are both lazy and take jobs away from local people. Here the other is seen as someone who lies around doing nothing, benefiting from a system that will

> **More often than not, the reasons we reject another arise after the actual rejection.**

care for him, *and* as someone who works harder and for less money than others to ensure that local people can't get jobs. These mutually exclusive claims (that they are lazy *and* work harder) show how the immigrant population is already hated, with reasons for the hatred being made up after the fact.

From this tribal perspective, the birth of Christianity is often understood as the birth of yet another worldview, another cultural group that takes its place beside all the others. Christianity thus takes its place beside every other division, as shown in the diagram below:

Tribal Separation

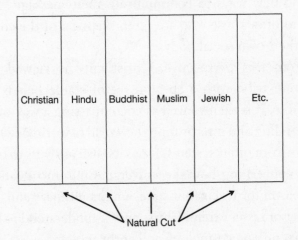

Here a distinction is drawn between those who believe in the Christian message and those who don't. Within the conservative vision of universalism, the mission of the church is then to encourage people to step from one side of the divide into the other, while the liberal universalist is happy to bide her time, as the truth will one day be revealed to all that the Christian narrative is the correct one.

Often church communities develop contemporary styles of worship and new modes of communication in order to convince people to change their tribal allegiances. For instance, churches often encourage their more creative leaders to set up alternative worship services that meet in coffee shops or bars, services that employ a rich blend of contemporary musical styles, fashions, and reference points. These "seeker sensitive" communities strive to find new ways to communicate their message. They seek to draw those who are often skeptical of the church into their own social body.

From this perspective, Christianity is viewed as a concrete tribe with a specific set of stable beliefs and practices. It is then viewed as encompassing a way of understanding and interpreting the world (a worldview) that differs from other systems. It has its own answers to questions concerning how the universe came into existence, the reason for its current state, and its ultimate end. To a greater or lesser extent, Christianity is understood to have its own unique cosmology and anthropology.

I Do Not Bring Peace, but a Sword

The natural cut that divides these various tribes, however, obscures a more fundamental cut, which is introduced by the apostle Paul. This cut is not one that separates one tribe from another, but one that creates a separation *within* tribes. Paul writes about this in Galatians 3:28: "There is neither Jew nor Gentile, neither slave nor free, neither male nor female, for you are all one in Christ Jesus." Here Paul mentions six distinct tribal identities that were ubiquitous in his time. Six identities that can be further subdivided into three, namely the religious (Jew and Gentile), the political (slave and free), and the biological (male and female).

Tribal Separation in Paul's Day

Religious		Political		Biological	
Jew	Gentile	Slave	Free	Male	Female

Natural Cut

It was not that these different groupings were totally isolated from one another, but the way that each of these groups related to the others was clearly defined and carefully regulated. The distinctions informed people whom they could interact with, how those interactions were to take place, and what freedoms were allowed.

These distinctions were justified by the authorities either in terms of Natural Law or Divine Plan; thus, the differences in roles and responsibilities were nonnegotiable and were required to maintain social stability.

One of Paul's radical insights was that he did not see the event of Christ as simply another identity to place alongside the others. Instead, he wrote of a different type of cut, one that cuts across all these concretely existing identities. In an unprecedented move, he wrote of how those who identify with Christ are no longer held captive by these categories, something we can signify in the following way:

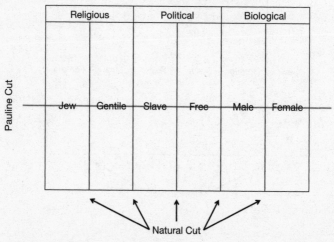

The Pauline Separation

Holding as if You Do Not Hold

For Paul, this new cut is the direct outworking of identifying with Christ, for in Christ we are confronted with one who gave up his identity out of love. The point here is not that you somehow cease to be identified with one of these groups, but that this new collective exists within the old order and brings you into contact with others previously seen as "outsiders."

One's concrete identity continues to exist, but it is now held differently and does not dictate the scope and limitations of one's being. Paul expresses this powerfully when he writes:

What I mean, brothers and sisters, is that the time is short. From now on those who have wives should live as if they do not; those who mourn, as if they did not; those who are happy, as if they were not; those who buy something, as if it were not theirs to keep; those who use the things of the world, as if not engrossed in them. For this world in its present form is passing away.*

What we witness here are concrete references to three different categories: (1) relationships, (2) the things that happen to us, and (3) the things we own. For Paul, these continue to exist, but we are to hold them differently than

---

*1 Corinthians 7:29–31

we previously had. We are no longer to act as though we are defined by the things we own, the things that happen to us, or by the relationships we have. While these continue to be important, we must hold them in a way that ensures they do not have an inescapable grasp upon us.

Paul understands this radical cut as emanating directly from one's identity with Christ, for Paul understands participation in the life of Christ as involving the loss of power that our various tribal identities once held for us. This concept is powerfully expressed in the theological meaning of the Incarnation. For in the Incarnation we are presented with a picture of God coming down to earth to take the very form of a human being and a servant. This is called kenosis and describes the act of self-emptying. This is most vividly expressed in the Crucifixion, where we see Christ occupying the place of the complete outsider, embracing the life of one who is excluded from the political system, the religious community, and the cultural network.

> **Paul understands this radical cut as emanating directly from one's identity with Christ.**

Indeed in the recorded ministry of Jesus, we find a multitude of references to one who challenged the divisions that were seen as sacred, divisions between Jew and Gentile, slave and free, and male and female. Jesus spoke to tax collectors, engaged with Samaritans, and treated women as equals in a world where these were outrageous acts. We see the rupturing of seemingly intractable divisions powerfully expressed in the following passage:

Leaving that place, Jesus withdrew to the region of Tyre and Sidon. A Canaanite woman from that vicinity came to him, crying out, "Lord, Son of David, have mercy on me! My daughter is demon-possessed and suffering terribly."

Jesus did not answer a word. So his disciples came to him and urged him, "Send her away, for she keeps crying out after us."

He answered, "I was sent only to the lost sheep of Israel."

The woman came and knelt before him. "Lord, help me!" she said.

He replied, "It is not right to take the children's bread and toss it to the dogs."

"Yes it is, Lord," she said. "Even the dogs eat the crumbs that fall from their master's table."

Then Jesus said to her, "Woman, you have great faith! Your request is granted." And her daughter was healed at that moment.*

As a Gentile and a Canaanite, this woman would have been viewed as a direct descendent of ancient Israel's enemies. The structure of this tale resembles that of a

---

*Matthew 15:21–28

parable, in that it begins with an action that those original readers of the text would both understand and affirm. Jesus was a Jew, and his mission was to the Jewish people, not those on the outside.

The original readers of this Gospel would readily identify with the disciples' desire to send this woman away as well as agreeing with Jesus's harsh response. And yet the woman fights back; she demands to have a place at the table, even if it means eating the crumbs. Here Jesus is chastised and rewards her persistence. In response, he opens up his ministry to the woman, signified by the healing of her daughter. Here the initial hearers of the story would also be chastised, as they are confronted with the fact that the mission of Jesus is one that breaks down religious, racial, and class divides.

This is powerfully driven home in a parable where Jesus is recorded as comparing the heavenly kingdom to a great banquet:

> The kingdom of heaven is like a king who prepared a wedding banquet for his son. He sent his servants to those who had been invited to the banquet to tell them to come, but they refused to come. Then he sent some more servants and said, "Tell those who have been invited that I have prepared my dinner: My oxen and fattened cattle have been butchered, and everything is ready. Come to the wedding banquet."
>
> But they paid no attention and went off—one to his field, another to his business. The rest seized his

servants, mistreated them and killed them. The king was enraged. He sent his army and destroyed those murderers and burned their city.

Then he said to his servants, "The wedding banquet is ready, but those I invited did not deserve to come. So go to the street corners and invite to the banquet anyone you find." So the servants went out into the streets and gathered all the people they could find, the bad as well as the good, and the wedding hall was filled with guests.*

In this parable we are first introduced to the natural division that those who first heard this parable would easily recognize: namely, the division between those who should rightfully be at a wedding party and those who should not. Like so many parables, this one begins with what people would understand and accept. But then it turns common ideas on their head and introduces the reader to something that cuts across what we take to be natural and right. A genuinely new, shocking, and distinctly unnatural division is presented to us—one that emerges between those who want to come to the party, despite their tribal differences, and those who exclude themselves by wanting to hold tightly to them.

At this banquet the doors are thrown open to both "the good" (those the listener would have taken to be the Jewish community) and "the bad" (which would have

---

*Matthew 22:2–10

been taken to mean the Gentiles). Now Jew and Gentile are able to encounter one another beyond the rigid structures defined by tradition, and the seemingly impermeable distinction between "good" and "bad" is first blurred and then relocated.

In this new type of party, "the good" refers to those who are willing to accept the invitation and stretch across party lines, while "the bad" refers to those who so tightly cling to their own identity that they are not willing to encounter others, listen to them, or allow them to be an instrument of their further transformation. This is brought home in a very stark way in the closing verses of the parable:

> But when the king came in to see the guests, he noticed a man there who was not wearing wedding clothes. He asked, "How did you get in here without wedding clothes, friend?" The man was speechless.
>
> Then the king told the attendants, "Tie him hand and foot, and throw him outside, into the darkness, where there will be weeping and gnashing of teeth."*

While this individual came to the party, he was not willing to give up his distinctive identity, keeping his own garments instead of dressing in the wedding clothes. In his refusal to lay down his identity, he was thus expelled from the party. The ones who believe they are part of the inner

---

*Matthew 22:11–13

circle (the divinely ordained tribe) find themselves outside the tribe opened up in Paul's understanding of Christ.

The Conflict Within Tribes

This brings us to the other side of this Paulinian cut, namely the way in which it unifies people from differing tribes, while causing a separation between members of the same tribe. As we can see in the diagram below, the cut is one that slices across the different identities that Paul presents. We see that there is a separation between those who dwell above the Paulinian cut and those who exist below it.

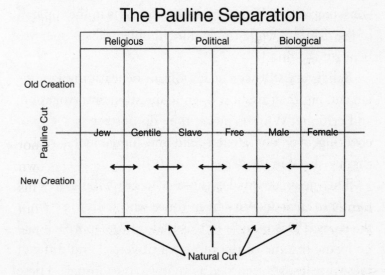

The Pauline Separation

Here we see, via the arrows in the bottom half of the diagram, that the community described by Paul is one in which those beneath the line have more in common with people from different social, religious, and biological positions than with people within their own community.

One could find that she agrees with almost everything that another in the community believes and yet find herself closer to a person who believes virtually none of the same things. The reason is straightforward: the two people from the same tribe hold the same beliefs, but the one above the Paulinian cut holds them differently than the one below that cut. While one grasps on to her beliefs as eternal and true, the other sees them as a provisional shelter that helps her navigate the world without allowing her to cover over a fundamental unknowing and genuine openness to others. In this way the old universalism of conservative and liberal traditions remains in the top half of the diagram while the Paulinian universalism operates beneath the line.

Beliefs are still seen as important beneath the Paulinian cut, but they are now open to question, interrogation, and critique. What is more, they do not act as a way of covering over our anxiety and the fundamental reality that we dwell in mystery.

This new cut divides those who are willing to hold lightly to their identity from those who wish to retain it at all costs. It is in light of this that we can approach and understand some of the most controversial and difficult ideas that Jesus is recorded as saying in the Gospels. These sayings revolve around Jesus's talk of bringing a sword into the world. Not a sword that would divide one group from another, but a sword that would make a cut within groups:

> **This new cut divides those who are willing to hold lightly to their identity from those who wish to retain it at all costs.**

> Do not suppose that I have come to bring peace to the earth. I did not come to bring peace, but a sword. For I have come to turn a man against his father, a daughter against her mother, a daughter-in-law against her mother-in-law—a man's enemies will be the members of his own household. Anyone who loves their father or mother more than me is not worthy of me; anyone who loves their son or daughter more than me is not worthy of me. Whoever does not take up their cross and follow me is not worthy of me. Whoever finds their life will lose it, and whoever loses their life for my sake will find it.*

At the time of Jesus, much like today, the family was the primary social, religious, and political unit. It was the place where you learned to distinguish between the good and the bad, the clean and the unclean, us from them. It is into this tight tribal unit that the sword of Christ makes its initial impact.

---

*Matthew 10:34–39

In terms of Paul's distinctions, we may say that once this sword has passed through a community, things initially look no different. Individuals remain what they were before the cut. There is no change biologically (male or female), religiously (Jew or Gentile), or politically (slave or free). Yet nothing remains the same, for these identities are now drained of their operative power and no longer hold us in the way they once did. These identities no longer need to separate us from one another and instead become more fluid and exhibit plasticity.

This cut is thus much more radical than the natural cuts that separate one tribe from another, for it breaks apart these natural separations and knocks down the walls we love to build.

Here we see how the sword of Christ spoken of in the Gospels cuts into the very heart of all tribal allegiances, bringing unity to what was previously divided while dividing what had once been unified. It is a sword that divides those who believe the same thing while bringing unification to those who may well believe very different things.

Those who are excluded from the new collective signaled by the new creation are now those who exclude themselves—the ones who so wish to cling to their own identity that they are not prepared to encounter another as anything but a stranger to convert, an alien to tolerate, or an enemy to crush.

Identifying with the One
Who Loses Identity

For Paul it is this very loss of identity that identifies us with Christ. As we experience the loss of the operative power of our identity, we thus touch upon that experience of utter loss expressed in the Crucifixion of Christ.

Those who dwell above the Paulinian cut justify themselves, either implicitly or explicitly, through some relation to an absolute that guarantees one's world and renders it safe (such as God, Destiny, Fate, Historical Necessity)—a guarantee that solidifies a person's identity and prevents him or her from truly encountering the other.

Above the Paulinian cut, seen in the previous diagrams, communication with others takes the form of consumption, vomiting out, toleration, or seeking out basic agreement. As we have previously explored, each of these tribes only engages the others to the level that their differences have been domesticated, ignored, or eradicated.

The other's difference must be avoided because it is a threat to the smooth running of our own beliefs. However, in contrast to the religious system, the new collective represented by those below the line can be described as religionless, insomuch as one's identity is experienced as provisional, ungrounded, and permeated by unknowing. This way of relating to our identity allows us to hold lightly to our tribal commitments and truly encounter others outside our own cultural, religious, and political narrative. Here God is not approached as an object that we must love, but as a mystery present in the very act of love itself.

We Are More Than the Story We Tell Ourselves

At one point Paul provocatively described Christians as the trash of the world (1 Corinthians 4:13). In other words, like rubbish, that which dwells outside, that which does not have a place within the walls. Christians were thus understood to be the excremental remainder that existed outside the social body, outside the various concrete identities of the day. They were that which did not have a place inside the body.

Instead of the conservative and liberal understanding of universalism as that which brings us into some concrete identity, the universalism of Paul invites us into a new type of collective, one in which we are liberated from the rigid nature of a particular identity. Both the conservative and liberal understanding of universalism simply offer the same logic we find in every other tribe, for both seek to retain their particular worldview as true. In contrast, the universalism that is captured in the idea of the Christian as the trash of the world invites us to identify with the one who is placed outside all systems. The one who identifies with Christ thus stands outside the very tribal systems that seek to define them. As a result we are being asked to give up the sense of mastery that our

> **The one who identifies with Christ thus stands outside the very tribal systems that seek to define them.**

traditions offer and open them up to the white-hot fires of unknowing and mystery. This is a universal message because we all are invited to join this liberated collective of nobodies and nothings. More than this, those who are already a part of this no-part are commissioned to preach this Goods News to the very ends of the earth.

CHAPTER 6

The Fool Says in His Heart, "There Is Knowing God"

The Horns of a Dilemma

It is not enough for us to merely identify how the event of Christ offers freedom from our zombie-like attachment to Idolatry and from the addiction to certainty that prevent us from embracing the mystery of existence and complexity of life. Understanding the oppressive system of Idolatry and Unbelief does not free us from it; the abstract recognition of our prison does not cause the bolted doors to open.

Understanding the basic structure of oppression and seeing a different possibility has little transformative power. We may acknowledge that we are caught in a system in which we seek something that will not satisfy us, and that we grasp certainty in order to repress our anxiety; or we may mock this system and ridicule people's involvement with it. But this will not affect our ongoing material commitment to it.

We cannot break free using our intellect because we did not intellectually enter into this system. It is what defines the very texture of our being, and so the only way out is through a change at the very core of our being, something that the apostle Paul called becoming a new creation: "Therefore, if anyone is in Christ, the new creation has come: The old has gone, the new is here!" (2 Corinthians 5:17).

This is nothing less than the description of a way of life in which we are no longer conformed to the structures and thinking of this world, something that Paul calls elsewhere the "renewing of your mind" (Romans 12:2).

In Christianity, we are not offered a form of thinking that might liberate us from the structure of this world—instead, the earliest Christian writings testify to the possibility of stepping into a different type of life, one in which we are free from this structure. These ancient writings hint at an event that offers us freedom from the obsessive drive for that which we (falsely) believe will

> The earliest Christian writings testify to the possibility of stepping into a different type of life, one in which we are free from this structure.

make us complete and from the mythologies that give us a (false) sense of mastery.

In the Gospels, Jesus is given the name "the second Adam." If the first Adam represents the order of slavery to Idolatry, then this image of Christ testifies to the possibility of a new creation, one that moves beyond the Idol and Unbelief. In order to understand how the Christ event testifies to this new creation, we must begin by understanding how Christ is initially understood by the believer.

For those of us trapped in the system of Idolatry and Unbelief, Christ is initially understood as the way in which we can grasp certainty and satisfaction. Thus to "believe" in Christ initially means that we fully embrace him as the ultimate Idol with whom we wish to be reunited. Here we substitute all possible gods for Jesus Christ, who becomes the very embodiment of the Idol and the guarantee that we are part of the right tribe.

This represents the first stage of Christian faith. Here Jesus is not that which frees us from our oppression to the Idol and Unbelief but is the ultimate expression of it (that which will make us whole and provide secret knowledge).

In order to understand the process, let us take a fictional example of a man named Finn—an example that will hopefully enable us to see how the event of Christ might be able to free us from the oppression of certainty and satisfaction.

Let us begin by imagining that Finn has recently experienced a conversion to Christianity. He has undergone a fundamental transformation and now attends church regularly. As a result he has lost interest in many of the things that once held him in rapture and is totally in love with Jesus. Finn has forsaken all for his newly found faith. He now considers himself a captive to Christ, a captivity that he experiences as profoundly freeing.

But over time, things begin to change. His initial joy seems a little more remote than it did at the beginning, and he is increasingly beset with questions about the beliefs that he once took for granted. He tries to pray more in order to rekindle his passion, and he reads some apologetics to bolster his beliefs, but neither seems that effective.

At this point, Finn has a choice to make. He has noticed that many of his friends have gone through similar experiences and notes that they tend to take one of two paths. He sees that some have made the difficult decision of leaving the church. They have renounced their Christianity as a type of delusion and begun to create a life for themselves outside the walls of the community that once meant so much to them.

In contrast, others seem to have repressed their questioning and insulated themselves from the outside world. They have few, if any, friends outside the community and read only material that agrees with the perspective they already hold. Unlike the first set of friends, who have left their Christianity behind, these people seem desperate to hold on to what they have at all costs.

For Finn, the encounter with other worldviews and

ideas has caused him to question his own. It seems that now he has only two real options: (1) reject his religion or (2) repress his doubts. The difficulty is that neither path seems that inviting—or, from a different perspective, they are both inviting for different reasons.

Rejecting Christ Is Not Too Extreme; It Is Not Extreme Enough

Let us imagine that Finn cannot bring himself either to walk away from his belief in God or repress all the doubts he has. Conflicted about what to do, he meditates on the Crucifixion of Christ until something breaks within him. In the midst of all his inner conflict, he suddenly feels a release. When he tries to describe the experience, all he can say is that it was as if God had touched him lovingly on the shoulder and whispered, "It's okay, you don't have to stop believing in me; I have stopped believing in myself."

Here Finn neither rejects the Idol nor continues to affirm it. Rather, that which he treats as the Idol falls apart from within. We see this play out at various times in the Christian scriptures when people keep wanting to treat Jesus as a type of king. In contrast, he is constantly depicted as doing things that undermine this idolatrous way of relating to him. Showing weakness when people expect strength, powerlessness when they want power, and humility when they want majesty. In other words, we believe in Jesus (as the Idol) and Jesus informs us that this is not the case.

To understand how this works, let's imagine that we believe having a luxury car will somehow bring us fulfillment. Let us assume that this belief has some operative power in our life.

It is not enough for us to reject this belief intellectually, for that will simply manifest itself in depression, in disguised hatred of those who have what we want (dressed up in a moral critique), or in a deeply felt dissatisfaction with what we are currently driving.

We uncouple ourselves from the belief not when we stop believing in it, but when we feel that those selling us the dream stop believing in it. Or, to put in more precise terms, we undergo change only when we are confronted with the car telling us that she won't bring us fulfillment.

It is not when we reject the Idol that we are freed from it but rather when we are directly confronted with the Idol rejecting its status as an Idol.

> **It is not when we reject the Idol that we are freed from it but rather when we are directly confronted with the Idol rejecting its status as an Idol.**

Only then is the system of oppression broken. The Cross testifies to a liberating logic where the prison of Idolatry is shattered from within. Like an egg that has been hollowed out, the system that enslaves us collapses in on itself. It is this that we witness in the words of Christ on the Cross: "It is finished." Here, as we undergo the event testified to in the Crucifixion, we experience the end of the old creation (the Temple curtain being ripped open to reveal nothing) and the beginning of the new (a life beyond the law).

If Finn were to leave Christianity when he begins to suspect that it cannot deliver what he originally imagined, he would end up replacing one Idol with another, for the structure itself has not been rejected. Here Idolatry is not broken but simply reshaped. The previous absolute belief could be replaced by a political agenda, a belief in wealth or any number of other things.

In contrast, if Finn holds on to his Idolatrous form of faith, he will be tempted to embrace that huge industry dedicated to conferences, worship concerts, and traveling apologists in an attempt to prop up the system that he clings to. The problem with these responses is that they both fail to grasp the truly radical move found in Christianity.

Making the Crucifixion into a Comedy

This experience of being inside the temple of Idolatry while it collapses in upon itself is deeply distressing and one that we attempt to avoid at all costs. We want to either reject one temple in favor of another or accept the one that we are in and work to fix the cracks. It is profoundly difficult to remain within a structure that collapses in on itself.

But the moment we experience the ground beneath our feet dissolving and feel the loss of all certainties is the moment we touch upon the experience of the Cross.

Sadly, it is this very experience that the church today seems dedicated to protecting us from. Instead of participating in the Crucifixion, we act in much the same way as the emperor in the famous Hans Christian Andersen story "The Emperor's New Clothes."

This ancient moral tale speaks of a vain emperor who seeks to be dressed in only the very finest of clothes. In his pursuit of the greatest garment, he hires two tailors who assure him that they will make the finest outfit in the world, an outfit made from a fabric that will be invisible to anyone who is hopelessly stupid.

The tailors present the supposedly magical cloth to the emperor, who is unable to see anything. However, he does not admit to this for fear of looking stupid and pretends to be impressed by the quality. The emperor's ministers also pretend they can see the material so as not to look foolish or contradict the emperor.

The deceptive tailors wait a little while then claim to have finished the suit. They pretend to dress the emperor, who proceeds to march in front of his subjects. Everyone who sees him plays along with the charade except for a little child who is too young to know that he ought to play along. Instead of saying nothing, this child shouts out that the emperor is naked. The emperor is overcome with embarrassment but continues to pretend that everything is the same as before. However, the game is up and the charade is obvious to everyone. In this way he becomes a laughingstock to his subjects.

This is the same logic that is played out in the classic comedies of Laurel and Hardy. One of the recurring motifs in their work is a situation in which Oliver Hardy exhibits an excess of pride and arrogance, only to be made to look ridiculous by a situation created by Stan Laurel.

The comedy works because Hardy realizes but never accepts the reality of his humiliation. He either disavows it by attempting to ignore what is happening or represses it by refusing to fully acknowledge it. The comedy would not work for us if he began to cry and changed as a result of what happened or if he kept on going in the situation without folding his arms and saying "this is another fine mess you've gotten me into." In the former situation we would simply feel sorry for him, while in the latter, we would not know when to laugh. We need Hardy to realize his stupidity while refusing it for the joke to work. The comic effect is created by the fact that the person who is the brunt of the joke realizes his humiliation yet refuses to acknowledge it.

> **The comic effect is created by the fact that the person who is the brunt of the joke realizes his humiliation yet refuses to acknowledge it.**

The church today largely teaches us to act like Oliver Hardy when it comes to the

Crucifixion. While the Cross signals the loss of the Idol, the church today either teaches us to disavow the experience of the Cross (saying that we are not really losing that which we believe grounds us, gives us meaning and promises fulfillment) or shows us how to repress it effectively (obliquely acknowledging the experience at some abstract level while protecting us from its full realization).

These different approaches to the Crucifixion can be seen in the different strategies found in the theologically conservative and liberal traditions. The former tend to engage in the act of disavowal whereby they refuse even to acknowledge the logic of the Cross. Here we are confronted with churches in which self-questioning and the experience of divine absence are seen as some kind of sin to repent of, a failure to be addressed, or a test to overcome.

In the latter, the logic of the Cross is expressed intellectually among individuals, even affirmed as part of Christian life, but the traumatic psychological impact of such a view is held at bay via a rigid liturgical structure that enacts certainty, presence, and security (with songs of triumphalism, sermons that describe God as the garniture of meaning, and rituals that help people feel safe, something I discuss in more depth in my book *Insurrection*).

On Getting the Joke

For Hardy there is, however, another possible option when faced with the type of "fine mess" Laurel puts him in, one that would effectively break the vicious cycle. It is a response that we see play out in the UK series *The Office*, written and directed by Ricky Gervais.

In this series David Brent (Gervais), the main character, initially acts in much the same way as Hardy. While he perceives himself to be a brilliant boss, wise mentor, comedian, musician, intellectual, and all-around Renaissance man, the reality is very different. Instead, he is petty, arrogant, narcissistic, irritating, and generally offensive. While he has some awareness of these undesirable traits, he is unable to admit them to himself, which is most apparent when he lashes out at people after the veil has been lifted, defending himself and blaming others.

The comedic element of the show is largely mined from the gap that exists between David Brent's perception of himself and the reality. Brent thus acts as the primary comic foil of the series because of his inability to embrace the embarrassing situations he finds himself in.

Yet, unlike Hardy, Brent gradually begins to become aware of his deficiencies. Instead of being a mere comic figure, Brent is, at the end of the series, presented as a more tragic character, as he becomes more aware of the truth he has previously attempted to repress or disavow. We see that he is actually a lonely and forlorn man who is trying to avoid confronting this truth through grasping on to an unrealistic image of himself. We, the viewer, have always known this; the change is how we relate to him once we know that he knows.

As he begins to accept himself for who he is we see small but important changes in his life. He is gradually transformed from the comic figure that the viewer takes pleasure in laughing at and becomes someone the viewer sympathizes with and even roots for. As he begins to accept himself, he is finally able to get his staff to laugh with him (instead of at him) and even meets a woman who actually enjoys his company.

It is here that the series ends. David Brent is finally able to admit to being a comic figure and, as such, stops being the brunt of the joke. Thus becoming a character who the viewer is more likely to care about. It is in this act of accepting his tragic status, instead of repressing or disavowing it, that he is able to start accepting himself and find some peace.

The Crucifixion and the Comedy of Existence

In the same way, the believer is faced with the challenge of accepting the full horror of the Crucifixion, realizing that the frantic pursuit of the Idol is damaging and that holding on to our tribal identities at all costs is repressive.

This Crucifixion experience is a deeply humiliating one, for it means realizing that we have been caught up in a fiction, a fiction that has ruled our lives and caused us to act in detrimental and often embarrassing ways. While we are not directly responsible for this fiction, because it arises from the birth of selfhood, there is a sense in which we need to face up to it and adopt an attitude of responsibility toward it. For while we can't help being factories in which Idols are created and certainties clung to, what is actually produced or believed reflects decisions we have made.

Instead of getting the joke, we insist on being the brunt of it. We do not want to walk the narrow path that stretches into the unknown. And so we take the brightly lit paths of either disavowal or repression—not accepting what is happening or pushing it into the darkest recesses of our mind. In effect we become like the emperor who refuses to accept that he is naked.

> We do not want to walk the narrow path that stretches into the unknown.

This is one of the ways we can interpret the mocking faces of grotesques that adorn old church buildings (the demonic-looking creatures found most often on the sides of Gothic cathedrals). They are the audience who is laughing at how we do not face up to our situation, at how we mimic the logic of Laurel and Hardy movies. In contrast, the one who embraces Christ on the Cross is the one who gets the cosmic joke, the one who enters into the humiliating but ultimately free-ing experience, of accepting and embracing our human condition.

The Missing Link

It is only when we have been lifted out of the old cre-ation that we can begin to truly appreciate the portrait of Jesus that is actually found in the biblical text. It is only from the position of the new creation that Jesus the Christ can be seen as something other than the material embodiment of the false Idol and garniture of ultimate meaning.

It is from this post-Crucifixion standpoint that we can begin to appreciate what the early Gospel writers meant when they described Christ as fully human and fully di-vine. Let us take each of these in turn.

By saying that Jesus was without sin, the early church gave us the portrait of one who lacked the lack. In other words, we are presented with the idea of one who was not marked by Original Sin, who was outside the reach of the Law and thus not driven by the Idol. In short, someone who was not tainted by the drive for ultimate satisfaction. It is in light of this that we can begin to understand the radical nature of the early church's claim that Jesus was fully human.

At first this might seem to suggest that Jesus is *not* fully human; after all, Original Sin marks one of our most fundamental experiences. Yet it is precisely this experience of Original Sin that makes us inhuman, or *pre*-human. It is this sense of separation that prevents us from finding a peace with ourselves and those around us. It is this sense of separation, combined with the prohibition, that drives us to try to fill a void in our existence, a void that prevents us from fully embracing the life that we are.

So then, in the image of Jesus as fully human, we are confronted with the image of someone *unlike* us. It could be said that the missing link between our animal ancestors and humanity is not something to be excavated from the ground for one simple reason: we are the missing link. We are the bridge that links what went before us to the fully human.

This is why we must avoid the standard criticism of artistic depictions of the face of Jesus that present a seemingly otherworldly figure. While it is true that the otherworldly expression we find in many Renaissance depictions distance him from ourselves, the point is that the distance is not one that separates *him* from humanity but instead points to how *we* are separated from *our own* humanity. By seeing the calm expression on Christ's face, we are confronted by the inhumanity of our own face.

In Jesus we are invited to imagine one who is at peace with himself, the world, and that which grounds the world. This is not testimony to one who has overcome Idolatry, but of one who has not been touched by it. Jesus presents to us not a picture of ourselves, but a picture

of what it might mean
to be ourselves, to be
whole, to live without
the lack that marks our
being.

> **Jesus presents to us a picture of what it might mean to be ourselves, to be whole, to live without the lack that marks our being.**

If claiming that Jesus
is God means that we
are as distant from Jesus
as we are from the most distant star, then saying that Jesus
is human is like saying we are as distant from Jesus as we
are from the smallest quark.

Christ as Fully God

Because Jesus is portrayed as one without the founding
separation of Original Sin, this helps us understand what is
meant by the idea that Jesus is fully God. For without the
foundational loss called Original Sin, Jesus has no relation
to the false god that this loss engenders. Without Original
Sin, there is no sense of a gap and no fantasy that something lies on the other side that could finally fulfill us. Jesus
thus has no relation to the false Idol posited by religion.

Instead we bear witness to a different understanding
of the divine. Not as that which lies beyond the abyss
created by Original Sin, but as the ground from which
everything arises.

Jesus is presented to us as being at one with the source

of all that is. Here we glimpse the idea that God is not that which lies ahead of us as a distant being we must attempt to reconcile with, but must be approached as the depth or ground that we can come into contact with once we are freed from the Idolatry that holds us captive. We must approach God as that reality we encounter indirectly through a deep and committed love of the world itself.

By understanding the humanity and divinity of Jesus in this way, we can begin to see how the relation between them is not one of paradox but of parallax. "Paradox" describes a set of statements that, when considered together, lead to seeming logical inconsistencies. In contrast, "parallax" describes how the viewpoint of the observer influences the way in which one perceives the object. Take the example of light: when viewed in one way, it acts as a wave, but when viewed in a different way, it acts as a particle. It is then one and the same phenomenon even though it manifests itself in two different ways, depending upon how we approach it.

God Does Not Exist, Is Not Sublime, and Has No Meaning

In our obsession with that which lies on the other side of the separation generated by Original Sin and the Law, we fail to see how this generates a more subtle and insidious type of separation. For in our pursuit of our various Idols, we become disconnected from the world we are a part of. Our current life is treated as a means to an end instead of embraced as an end in itself.

In the Gospels we are presented with the image of a man who was at one with life, himself, and his surroundings. One who spoke out against those who would seek to keep people enslaved in Idolatry and told stories that always subverted the certainties of the day. It is in the aftermath of the Crucifixion that we are able to understand that the God revealed in Christ is found in the loving embrace of this life and a rejection of all that would turn us away from this.

In contrast to the Idol that we experience as existing, as sublime, and as meaningful, the God revealed in Christ, as present in the work of love, resists each of these characteristics. While the Idol is a fiction that we experience as existing, we may say that the God of Christ is a reality that we experience as *not* existing.

Instead, this God is present as the source that calls everything into existence. The word "exist" literally means "to stand out." The main characteristic of something that exists is that we are able to treat it as an object of some sort. We are able to hold it, contemplate it, smell it, touch it, or hear it. The God hinted at in Christianity is that which calls everything into existence, all the while defying objectification.

To understand what this means, think about walking along a busy street and coming upon someone you love. While walking you are passing hundreds of people, and yet you do not really "see" any of them. You perhaps register them as objects to avoid, but they do not stand out for you. However, when you see someone you love, she stands forth from the background. She arises from the formless mass of others as distinct. With this in mind we may say that God is the name we give to that experience where things are called into existence for us. In this way, it can be said that God is not seen but is testified to in a particular way of seeing. Previously we saw how the Idol is experienced as existing, until we grasp it and discover that it doesn't. Here God is felt not to exist, and yet by this act of calling everything into existence it seems that the moment we stop trying to grasp God the existence of God is indirectly testified to in the existence of everything we encounter.

> God is not seen but is testified to in a particular way of seeing.

This brings us to the second aspect of God that is distinct from the Idol. The Idol is experienced as that which is utterly beautiful, that which is so radiant everything else pales into insignificance. But when we read that God is love, we are reminded that love cannot be directly approached as beautiful and sublime but as that humble reality that renders the world beautiful and sublime. Love does not say, "Look at me," but invites us to look at another. Unlike the Idol that tries to capture our gaze, the God testified to in love avoids our direct gaze and invites us to be taken up by the beauty that surrounds us. The Idol is seen as beautiful only until it is grasped and we discover the beauty was a fiction. In contrast, it would seem that as we stop trying to grasp God as beautiful we discover that the source of all beauty is indirectly discovered as beautiful in the beauty of all things.

Finally, the God revealed in the Christian scriptures differs from the Idol in that this God is not meaningful. The Idol we desire is not only meaningful to us, it is so singularly meaningful that everything else effectively becomes meaningless. In contrast, the God found in love is not meaningful but is that reality that renders the world meaningful.

When someone is in love he cannot help but experience the world as meaningful, even if he doesn't believe it is. While the one who does not love cannot help but experience the world as meaningless even if he believes that the world is meaningful. Love then infuses the world with meaning regardless of what one believes about it. By revealing God as love, the Christian tradition rejects the idea that God is a meaningful being in favor of the idea that God is that which lights up our world, rendering it meaningful to us. This means that unlike the Idol, which seems meaningful until grasped, the moment we lay down the idea of God as meaningful and find the world infused with meaning, we bear witness to the meaningfulness of the divine.

The point here is that we should avoid making the mistake of affirming the polar opposite of the proverb that states, "The fool says in his heart, 'There is no God.'" (Psalm 14:1) For Christianity does not assert that we can directly know God any more than it says there is no God. In Christ we are confronted with a different understanding altogether, one in which God is not directly known (either as a being "out there" or as found in all things), but is the source that renders everything known.

To make the claim that you know God is actually to proclaim a no-God. It is to proclaim an Idol, masked as God.

The categories of existence and nonexistence begin to break apart when speaking of God. The Idol is a fiction that we think exists, a meaningless object that we bestow with all meaning and a mundane object that we believe is sublime. In contrast we let go of existence, meaning, and the sublime as categories to describe the object "God." Instead these become ways in which we engage with the world. Yet, as we affirm the world in love, we indirectly sense that in letting go of God we have, in fact, found ourselves at the very threshold of God.

Christianity as Anti-Wisdom

In this way we can begin to understand why the apostle Paul is so against Greek philosophy, writing, "See to it that no one takes you captive through hollow and deceptive philosophy, which depends on human tradition and

the basic principles of this world rather than on Christ."
(Colossians 2:8)

During Paul's time, much like today, wisdom taught us that ascribing some kind of meaning to the world is irrational. In many ways the Christian tradition can be seen as a refusal to accept this wisdom. It should not be seen as a refusal to believe this wisdom any more than it should be seen as affirming it; it is simply a refusal to engage in the world in this way. The rejection of wisdom philosophy in Christianity is not, then, intellectual in nature, it is existential; it is a protest against living as if there is no meaning.

Love's refusal of wisdom is nothing less than the act of investing the world with purpose, beauty, and meaning, regardless of whether or not it merits such things. It involves bestowing mundane matter with a sense of wonder, seeing the movement of molecules as meaningful, and finding a sense of awe in the heart of life itself.

Love is a refusal of worldly wisdom in that it lives "as if." Not engaging in some philosophical discussion about whether this nihilistic view of the world is right or wrong, but embracing the world as that which is radiant, sacred, and sublime.

Love is the crazy, mad, and perhaps ridiculous gesture of saying yes to life, of seeing it as worthy of our embrace and even worthy of our total sacrifice.

> **Love is the crazy, mad, and perhaps ridiculous gesture of saying yes to life.**

The book of Ecclesiastes provides us with an insight into this way of life. Initially this text offers one of the bleakest visions of the world to be found in ancient literature, and yet it offers so much more for the careful reader.

The writer of Ecclesiastes was a man of great power who ruled over Israel. During his adult life he tells us that he put his energy into all the things that people do in order to find meaning and happiness. He embraced hedonism, the search for wisdom, the pursuit of beauty, and the betterment of society. Yet each time he found that they fell short of offering satisfaction and certainty. Each time he was haunted by the inevitability of death and the fact that he would be forgotten with the passage of time.

It is in this bleak vision that we see a foretelling of the Crucifixion. While Ecclesiastes is often treated as a marginal text by Christians, the teacher's cry—"Meaningless, meaningless, everything is meaningless"—resonates deeply with Christ's cry on the Cross: "My God, my God, why have you forsaken me?" For here we encounter the impotence of the Idol and the loss of mythological constructs.

The teacher of Ecclesiastes was able to describe this dark place because he had achieved everything that we might believe could make us happy and whole; he had broken through the obstacles and found nothing of substance on the other side. As each of these gods was exposed as impotent, Solomon realized what most never do: that this whole system is a farce.

Yet the book does not leave us in this place of despair,

for dotted throughout the pages is a hint at what we discover in the event of Resurrection. For the writer keeps coming back to the theme of embracing and valuing life. At different times he mentions the importance of enjoying what we eat and drink, our work, and our possessions. For instance, we read:

> This is what I have observed to be good: that it is appropriate for people to eat, to drink and to find satisfaction in their toilsome labor under the sun during the few good days of life God has given them—for this is their lot.
>
> Moreover, when God gives people wealth and possessions, and the ability to enjoy them, to accept their lot and be happy in their toil—this is a gift from God. They seldom reflect on the days of their lives, because God keeps them occupied with gladness of heart. (Ecclesiastes 5:18–20)

Immediately after this, we read of those who possess everything they could possibly want and yet who still cannot affirm life:

> I have seen another evil under the sun, and it weighs heavily on the human race: God gives some people wealth, possessions and honor, so that they lack nothing their hearts desire, but God does not grant the ability to enjoy them, and strangers enjoy them instead. This is meaningless, a grievous evil.

A man may have a hundred children and live many years; yet no matter how long he live, if he cannot enjoy his prosperity and does not receive proper burial, I say that a stillborn child is better off than he. It comes without meaning, it departs in darkness, and in darkness its name is shrouded. Though it never saw the sun or knew anything, it has more rest than this man—even if he lives a thousand years twice over but fails to enjoy his prosperity. (Ecclesiastes 6:1–6)

The truth that is hinted at here is the idea that love is what brings meaning. The one who loves life and embraces others finds meaning in even the most mundane of activities. Food is no longer about sustaining the body but of communing with others, drinking does not simply satisfy a thirst but joins people in celebration, work is not about achieving some future happiness but about filling one's present with worthwhile activity.

> The one who loves life and embraces others finds meaning in even the most mundane of activities.

The problem, however, is that the book of Ecclesiastes does not fully enter into the understanding of God found in the Resurrection. If the message of Ecclesiastes is that everything is meaningless but we can still find solace in embracing our life, then the message of the Resurrection is that the categories of meaning and meaninglessness are part of an old order that has been superseded by a new one.

The way of Resurrection opens up a different type of understanding, one that is not affirmed intellectually but lived. An understanding that can only truly be grasped once one has been freed from the old order of Idolatry and Unbelief.

The writer of Ecclesiastes got as close to the truth as one can without actually being pulled out of the old creation and birthed into the new one. Hence there is still a deep melancholy in this philosophical treatise that is lacking in the joyous life testified to in Resurrection. We see this joy in the life of Jesus, who was at one with the source out of which everything arose and thus was able to embrace life, even in the darkest hour—enjoying a meal with his friends when he knew that he would soon be executed.

To go through the event of Crucifixion does not then mean that we are unified with that which will make our lives complete, nor that we are given some secret knowledge that will abolish our ignorance, but that we can live without being complete and can celebrate mystery instead of being afraid of it. Not only is the fiction of gaining certainty and satisfaction exposed in the Crucifixion and Resurrection, but more importantly, the Crucifixion and Resurrection are names we give to the freedom from these oppressive fictions.

As Christ dies on the Cross we read of the tombs breaking open and the dead coming to life. Why? Because it is here that the death-dealing structure of Idolatry and Unbelief is broken apart and a new mode of life erupts. A life in which the source of all is no longer approached as some being whom we ought to love, but as a mystery we participate in through the very act of love itself.

Part Three

_____

THE NEW
COLLECTIVE

CHAPTER 7

I Need Your Eyes in
Order to See Myself

Encountering Our
Own Monstrosity

After exploring how we are caught up in a relentless
pursuit of certainty and satisfaction and showing how
the early Christian writings testify to a way of living free
from them, we must now turn our attention to how this
might be expressed in community. What would a group
seeking to enter into and remain faithful to such a way of
life actually look like?

The name that we give to the community attempting
to press into the way of life expressed in Christ is called

the church. And yet the church in its present form seems caught up in the very prison of seeking certainty and satisfaction that the Christ event abolishes. Mythological thinking and the idea of God as product are rife in the very place that we should expect the opposite. The task at hand is thus huge, for it involves rethinking the very nature of church from the ground up.

What follows is a brief sketch of how one group has liturgically enacted the ideas explored in the last two sections. My hope is that you will find something in these pages that is either directly applicable to your own situation or useful as you explore different ways to evoke and remain faithful to the way of life explored thus far.

We have already looked at the tendency to judge those who are "other" than ourselves, deciding whether they are right or wrong by simply comparing their views to our own and seeing how similar they are. We spoke of the strategies of *consumption* (where we seek to integrate the other into our social body), *vomiting* (where we reject the one we cannot integrate), *toleration* (where we accept the other insofar as we are not directly confronted by their difference), and *agreement* (where we find points of commonality and focus on them).

Consumption and vomiting are the primary responses to the other that we see arising from a conservative position, while toleration and agreement are what we find embodied in a liberal position. For in the conservative vision, the other can only be integrated or relegated to the category of lost, while in the liberal approach, the other's difference can be tolerated or largely ignored, as they will eventually come to know the truth.

In contrast to these, we mentioned a fifth response, namely that of placing ourselves into question through the presence of the other. This gets us to the heart of the universalism described by the apostle Paul. As we have explored, for Paul, the Christian is one who experiences his tribal identity as a mask that prevents him from confronting the anxiety of unknowing.

One of the primary ways that we can enter into this new collective described by Paul is through a genuine encounter with someone whose beliefs, practices, or desires are different from our own. As a concrete example of this in my own life, one evening, when I was much younger, I was in the pub with a group of friends. I can't remember now what the conversations were, but I do remember one point where a person said, "That is so gay" to a comment from one of those in the group. This comment was then jokingly repeated a number of times at various points in the evening with my implicit approval.

A few days later, I happened to be out with one of the people who was part of that group. We were just catching up when he stopped midsentence, looked right at me, and said, "Pete,

> We can enter into a type of Paulinian universalism through a genuine encounter with someone whose beliefs, practices, or desires are different from our own.

I am gay. Can you imagine how I felt when everyone started using the term 'gay' in such a negative way the other night?"

At that moment I was undone. I wanted to defend myself by pointing out my disgust with homophobia. Instead I was brought to silence. I saw myself through the eyes of my friend, and I was shocked by what I saw. It was only because I was given grace and understanding that I was able to face myself in that moment.

So often we avoid confronting our own prejudices by covering them over and avoiding anyone who might expose them. But it is the other who so often holds the key to our development. Not by presenting us with something we do not know, but by presenting us with something we do know (insomuch as we live it out) but refuse to acknowledge.

It is in this genuine encounter with the other that our own unseen issues begin to break down. In the other we are brought to the place where we must question whether we can begin to see the shadow side of our beliefs.

On Pretending to Meet the Other

It is easy to see how we seek to protect ourselves from a genuine encounter with others. While some unapologetically embrace their worldview as absolute truth and are not open to listening to others, most of us engage in more subtle means of insulating ourselves. We are often keen to point out that we are open to listening to others and learning from people who come from different traditions. We will be happy to say that we have beliefs but will often follow that by saying that we are open to learning, changing, and developing.

These claims, however, must be tested against how we live, for they may turn out to be similar to the claims of someone with an alcohol problem saying that he is not really an alcoholic. In order to understand this, let us take a concrete example. Recently there was a popular Christian project that set up a type of confessional booth in a university campus. The difference between this booth and the typical confessional booth was that instead of people confessing their sins to the Christians who set it up, the Christians confessed the sins of the church to the people who came to the booth. Initially this can seem like a genuine attempt to hold more lightly to one's own position. However, on closer inspection, this act, while good in some ways, does not place the Christian's ideology into question but only the parts that were seen to fall short of that ideology. The evils generally reflected only those that are now taken by most rational people to have been crimes against individuals and groups. In this way the group was able to protect itself from the terrifying experience of being wrong at the level of foundational beliefs while seemingly being open through admitting that they fall short of these.

This achieves two objectives. First, the Christians in

the booth could feel humble and open to admitting their failings as an historical body. Second, it made for a more effective evangelism strategy. In short, this act did not demonstrate that they were holding their beliefs lightly but actually allowed those who participated to hold on to their tribal identity just as strongly as before. It allowed the Christian community to maintain their tribal identity while experiencing a domesticated sense of openness to the other.

One way we can begin to work out whether we are domesticating our encounters with others is to reflect on what we read, whom we engage seriously with, and who our friends are. When we take a step back and look at our actions (checking our bookshelves, calendars, and social media networks), do we not find that we stay mainly with those people who think like us? Do we read books that confirm our already held positions, listen to programs that already take a position close to our own, read journalists who solidify our own political and religious allegiances? And if we do engage with people who are different from ourselves, is it in a highly regulated and safe environment? For example, when reading about people we disagree with, do we read their words from books in which the author is critiquing them? Or if

> When we take a step back and look at our actions, do we not find that we stay mainly with those people who think like us?

we do spend time with people who hold different views of the world, is it because we are forced to (sharing a job or place of study), engaging with the other only as long as they keep their views hidden from us?

The Dis-Courses

So how can we actually encourage a genuine encounter with others, one that can cause a feedback loop that short-circuits our fantasy that we stand upon a timeless, historical, eternal truth? How do we create the space where we are truly able to rupture the defense mechanisms that are designed to protect us from an encounter with the other so that we can glimpse the poverty of the narratives we construct, important though they are? In short, how can we begin to fracture the fortresses of certitude that we have built?

It could be said that humans have always sought, in different ways, to be God. It is natural for us to want to escape our finitude, to have the answers, to gain a God's-eye view of the universe. But interestingly, within the Christian narrative, becoming like God would mean embracing our humanity. For this is what we see in the Incarnation. Becoming like God would mean affirming our finitude, celebrating our limits, and accepting that we are immersed in mystery. These are not signs that we've somehow failed to touch the heart of faith; instead, facing their reality demonstrates courage and faith. Indeed, it is a sacred act that is not something we do *to* our faith but is an expression *of* our faith.

When we accept our unknowing and brokenness, we are not weakening our faith, we are boldly expressing it. It is our faith that brings us into this place of accepting humility and acknowledging our limits.

For the practitioner, creating spaces where we can talk about these issues is not enough. The challenge is to create environments where the experience is undergone. In other words, the task is to form collectives that invite people into this revelatory rupture. In practice, this means we must find a way for people to encounter perspectives different from their own in an environment where they are encouraged to listen and engage. Not simply to learn about the other, but to see themselves through the eyes of the other and thus encounter their own historicity.

These collectives will take many forms, but I wish to spend a little time in this chapter exploring two contemplative practices dedicated to this goal. These practices are designed to rupture the power of our mythological narratives so that we are better able to glimpse the truth they obscure.

These practices, together with the ones I will outline in the following chapter, can be called *dis-courses* because they are designed to send people off their present course and onto a new one.

These dis-courses were developed from the conviction

that while the experiences of doubt, unknowing, openness to the other, and the sense of divine absence are profoundly sacred, they are also deeply troubling. It is always difficult when our political, religious, and cultural views are placed into question, because they have helped to found our sense of self. Thus we need powerful contemplative practices designed to walk us through the experience.

The Last Supper

The first contemplative practice I want to look at is called the Last Supper and received its inspiration from a film directed by Stacy Title of the same name. The aim of the group is simply to provide a space for participants to meet and interact with someone whose political, religious, and/or social views diverge from their own.

The format is straightforward. Roughly twelve people gather together in a room for a meal. A guest is invited to address the group, someone with views and opinions that would likely differ from most of the people attending. The guest is introduced during the starter, then, during the main meal, she gives a short talk on the theme of her choice. Over dessert, people can ask questions and interrogate some of the ideas that have been presented. Then, during coffee or after-dinner drinks, a wider discussion ensues.

The event is playfully called the Last Supper because,

if the presenter does not prove convincing, we inform her that this could turn out to be her last supper.

There are very few guidelines for the evening, but a few "dinner manners" are recommended. The original Last Supper events had three guidelines that were printed on coasters and placed around the table. The first encouraged everyone to participate in the conversation. The second asked that people try not to dominate the conversation, while the third invited everyone to be open to different perspectives.

The idea of the Last Supper as a contemplative practice is to draw people into an experience of learned ignorance, i.e., a type of ignorance that does not come from a lack of engagement with ideas but one that comes from an active engagement. This experience rarely comes about through a one-time event; rather, people are encouraged to commit to a series of these dinners over the course of a year. One event will simply be interesting, but a series of events can weave together in a way that can bring about real change of the type we have been describing.

> The idea of the Last Supper as a contemplative practice is to walk people into an experience of learned ignorance.

The Evangelism Project

One of the strengths of the Last Supper lies in the way that there is one guest to twelve participants. This allows people who have rarely engaged with someone different from themselves to do so in a safe environment. However, there is also a limitation, for the environment could be seen to be a little too safe for those who would like to be challenged in a deeper way. With that in mind we can turn to a second contemplative practice called the Evangelism Project.

The Evangelism Project involves bringing people to different religious, political, and cultural communities, not to evangelize them, but to be evangelized. Each visit is made up of three elements: the first involves witnessing the activities of the group being visited, the second is made up of a conversation about the beliefs and practices of the group, while the final element gives those involved in the Evangelism Project the opportunity to ask how they look to the community they are visiting.

The aim of the practice is to provide those attending with a way of encountering the alien beliefs and practices of others in order to discover the alien nature of their own beliefs and practices.

The "good news" of the Evangelism Project is not that those involved will be converted by the group being visited but that by seeing themselves through the others' eyes, they might begin to see things in themselves that were previously repressed.

When we first encounter someone who is different from ourselves, we are confronted with a gap that exists between us and them, a space that separates us from the other. But the contemplative practice of the Evangelism Project is designed to draw out a more unnerving gap. Not one that exists between "us" and "them," but a gap that exists within ourselves. For when we genuinely look at how the other sees us, we are confronted with a distance that exists between the image we have of ourselves and the reality of our actions. As with the Last Supper, the Evangelism Project is a contemplative practice that helps us encounter someone who is alien to us so that we can experience the insight that we are alien to ourselves. Like the Last Supper, people need to commit to this practice over a prolonged period of time for it to have a significant and lasting effect.

It is difficult for us to experience the reality that how we perceive things is directly connected to a variety of biological and cultural factors. We may, for instance, find a certain experience scary or painful and take it for granted that any "normal" person would feel the same way, only to find that others do not. It is not unlike the way many of us consume the news. It is natural for us to view the camera that broadcasts images as a type of window into the world, i.e. a broadly objective, untainted lens into what is taking place. Exposure to how news is constructed, however, teaches us that this is not the case; that the way the camera is used (what it shows and doesn't show), along with the commentary and the context, provides the viewer with a particular point of view. The fact that television offers us a tainted perception of what is really going on is merely a derivative and secondary experience that covers over a more radical truth—that we offer ourselves a tainted perspective of what is really going on.

In both the Evangelism Project and the Last Supper, participants begin to experience this truth because they are decentered by their encounter with difference. Thus, the transformation that takes place does not primarily occur as a result of a direct encounter with the beliefs of the other but via an encounter with the gaze of the other that brings us face-to-face with our own beliefs.

CHAPTER 8

Destroying Christianity and Other Christian Acts

We Do Not Doubt Our Faith; To Doubt Is an Expression of Our Faith

The power of contemplative practices like the Last Supper and the Evangelism Project lies in the way that they help us to encounter ourselves through an encounter with the other. In committing ourselves to these practices, we begin to experience our own beliefs and practices as simply one more identity that covers over the human condition. Christianity—insofar as it is reduced to simply one more political, cultural, or religious narrative—is unmasked as having the same status as the six categories that Paul wrote of in his day: Jew, Gentile, slave, free, male, and female.

In this way we can begin to approach the event testified to in Christianity as that which questions all such narratives. To put it differently, one doesn't simply deconstruct one's Christianity, for this very act of deconstruction is a direct expression of Christianity.

Fidelity to the Christian event thus means the commitment to experiencing a type of short-circuit in the various narratives we adopt.

Embracing the Enemy

We can begin to understand what this means as we consider the way in which every concrete belief system opens up the space for those who would deny it. This simply means that every worldview that is put forward can be critiqued and rejected. No matter how powerful and influential the worldview, some will eventually critique it and assert the opposite. Indeed, it is often the case that the more powerful and influential a worldview, the more sophisticated, passionate, and powerful its opposition will be.

In terms of religion every theistic system can be seen to have its atheistic opposite.

> **Every concrete belief system eventually gives birth to those who would deny it.**

There are as many atheisms as there are theisms. There is, for example, Jewish atheism, Buddhist atheism, Christian atheism, and Islamic atheism. All of which are slightly different, for each rejection is specifically geared to that which it is in opposition to.

Whenever a concrete community is first faced with their own negation, they will often reject those who reject them. Those who oppose them are treated as apostates (people who have abandoned the faith) or infidels (those who were never part of it) and attacked.

Over time, however, communities often develop ways of living with those who deny their worldview. This move from outright rejection to begrudging acceptance often begins simply because the opposition becomes too strong to destroy or persecute.

Eventually a third response often arises beyond forceful exclusion or begrudging tolerance. This third response involves communities getting to the point where they are willing to listen to and engage with those who reject their worldview. In this way the community, or certain parts of the community, actively engage with their opposition, viewing this confrontation as a way of sharpening, deepening, and developing their own ideas.

What each of these responses to opposition share in common is a sense of separation from the critique. In each the other is held at a distance, whether it is through persecution, tolerance, or even dialogue, the other is considered to be on the outside of the community.

In Christianity, however, we witness a different response, one that obliterates the separation that is caused by such opposition. In this different approach the critique is integrated into the very heart of affirmation itself. In other words, the critique is no longer seen as leading away from the faith or even as a way of sharpening it but instead as part of its deepest expression.

This is witnessed in various places in the biblical text; however, we see its clearest expression at the very heart of Christianity itself. For on the cross, when Christ cries out, "My God, my God, why have you forsaken me?" we see that the absence of God as object is brought into the very heart of the faith. Here the loss of God is seen to be part of the life of faith rather than its destruction. If a Christian is to participate in the Crucifixion, then that involves undergoing that felt absence. This is not an optional extra or a depressing experience that a few melancholy souls must endure: *it is a constitutive experience for the Christian.*

Instead of viewing those who claim that God is absent as enemies to fight, strangers to tolerate, or misguided friends to listen to, we are confronted with the possibility that they are expressing something of central importance to the Christian faith.

What follows are two practices that were created in order to draw out how the critique of Christianity as a system and the experience of divine absence are inherent parts of Christianity.

Atheism for Lent

The first contemplative practice is called Atheism for Lent and was inspired by the book *Suspicion and Faith* by the philosopher Merold Westphal, a text designed to introduce readers to some of the greatest critiques of Christianity.

Lent is a time that is traditionally reserved for a type of psychological purging that leads up to the Crucifixion. In light of this, the Atheism for Lent course seeks to use some of the most potent critiques of Christianity as a type of purifying fire that might help us appreciate and understand Christ's cry of dereliction on the Cross in a new way. Just as Christ experienced the loss of God as object on the Cross, so the Atheism for Lent course invites participants into that desert space traditionally called the dark night of the soul.

> Lent is a time that is traditionally reserved for a type of psychological purging that leads up to the Crucifixion.

In order to draw people into this, the practice of Atheism for Lent exposes participants to some of the greatest, most perceptive criticisms and critiques of God, religion, and faith, the hope being that this difficult and challenging journey will result in the destruction of Idolatrous ways of thinking about faith.

The format is quite straightforward; for each day of Lent there is a small reflection for people to read, watch, or listen to. Then once a week, everyone meets up together to discuss them with a facilitator over a meal. The material in question is drawn from thinkers like Feuerbach, Freud, Marx, and Nietzsche, as well as more contemporary sources such as the work of Daniel Dennett, Richard Dawkins, and Christopher Hitchens. In addition to this, the Atheism for Lent course benefits from the use of films, documentaries, and popular debates, all of which can be tailor made by the community committed to practicing this discipline.

The Omega Course

One of the limitations of Atheism for Lent lies in the way that it rests on critiques of Christianity that come from those who perceive themselves as outsiders. In light of this, the Omega Course was a practice designed to draw out how this kind of critique is alive and well in the debates going on within the Christian community.

The name of this faith practice was inspired by the large-scale evangelical project called the Alpha course. The Alpha course consists of ten meetings, along with an introductory session and a weekend retreat, and is designed to introduce people to some of the basic doctrines affirmed by the contemporary church. Each of the events takes place over a meal and involves a talk (often in the form of a video presentation) and discussion. Some of the subjects explored include who is Jesus, why did he die, what is faith, does prayer work, how to read the Bible, the nature of the Holy Spirit, and whether or not God intervenes in the world.

The Omega Course was designed to explore many of the same themes taken up by the Alpha course and do so in a similar manner (via video clips and discussion). However, while the Alpha course is designed to bring people into a form of doctrinally based Christianity, the Omega Course is designed to draw people away from such a mythological form of Christianity. It does not do this, however, by directly attacking a certain theological perspective; instead, it shows how there are a variety of perspectives within Christianity—perspectives that often stand in sharp contradiction to one another.

Unlike the Alpha course, the conversation is not directed to a conclusion in which people are encouraged to embrace the "right" doctrinal answer—instead, the conversation itself is what is deemed important. Disagreements are encouraged, and the passionate exchange of ideas is affirmed. By the end of the course, people thus experience firsthand that Christianity is not a singular, monolithic, unchanging belief system but a fluid tradition that is always interrogating itself.

During the course people get to see that in addition to minor differences in theological perspectives there are also huge, monumental shifts in the thought of the church—shifts that do not simply change what happens within a given theological frame but that transform the frame itself.

The Omega Course is not some relativistic space where the idea that there is some central truth to the universe is replaced with the idea that there is none (for this is just one more claim to absolute knowledge); instead, the practice draws out the possibility that the truth is not what lies on one side of the debate or the other, but is hinted at in the ongoing debate itself.

The evenings offer a safe space for people to be honest about their questions, beliefs, and doubts without feeling that they would be judged as a result of what they say. Through the various discussions and video clips, participants are exposed not only to the limits and problems with their own beliefs, but also to the idea that this acknowledgment is not a failure of faith but an expression of it.

The Mystery Within

Through undergoing the practices outlined in this chapter and the previous one, the hope is that individuals experience a radical shift in the location of mystery and unknowing. Initially we tend to think of mystery as that which we do not yet know. Mystery is the name we give to something that is "out there," something beyond us that arises because we lack the necessary data or capabilities. However, through the four practices we have looked at, individuals are confronted with a more disconcerting type of mystery. Not a mystery that lies *beyond* the world we understand but a mystery that lies *within* it.

> We are confronted with a more disconcerting type of mystery. Not a mystery that lies *beyond* the world we understand but a mystery that lies *within* it.

We can see an example of this difference when we compare classical science with quantum mechanics. In classical science there were two types of mystery. There was the mystery of things we didn't currently understand, and there was the mystery of the system itself. While there were any number of things in the universe that we did not grasp, it was broadly believed that there was nothing that could not, in principle, be known. In contrast, the second type of mystery lay in why the whole scientific enterprise worked in the first place. That the universe was elegant, ordered, and consistent seemed patently true due to the success of the scientific method, yet it was not something that could be directly understood by that method.

However, in quantum mechanics something radically different happened. Mystery now was no longer simply related to what we did not currently know or to the mysterious fact that the universe was knowable via the scientific method. With the work of scientists like Heisenberg, we discovered that mystery and unknowing were actually built into the structure of the universe itself. What Heisenberg discovered was that we could not know the momentum and the position of a particle at the same time. The more we knew about one, the less we could know about the other. In short, mystery was no longer related to something "out there" but was in the very fabric of everything.

We see this also in the Christian scriptures, for in them we witness a move from thinking of God as a mystery "up there," a being above and beyond us that we cannot grasp, to approaching God as a mystery in the midst. The point is not that the mystery of God is dissipated in the Incarnation, but that this mystery is brought into the heart of the world. The mystery now is in our midst. The unknowing is here dwelling among us. The unknowing hasn't dissipated; the mystery has been brought beyond the threshold, into the world.

In the same way, the Last Supper, the Evangelism Project, Atheism for Lent, and the Omega Course all exist to help us come into contact with the mystery and the unknowing that we are immersed in—an unknowing that we cannot get rid of, no matter how hard we study, indeed an unknowing that we feel ever more strongly as we study.

There are three final things we can note about these contemplative practices. First, they each derive from the Christian tradition. They are fed by that tradition, and they help us understand that tradition in a deeper way.

Second, these courses all run with the idea that we must take this journey into unknowing and immanent mystery rather than just intellectually affirm it. This dark night of the soul is not something we discuss and dissect but instead is a reality we are invited to enter into. And third, each of these practices is sustained by the idea that we must go through this traumatic, liberating event in community. For if we undergo this experience on our own, we will be in danger of falling into despair, depression and deep loneliness. We need other people as we take the journey described in this book; we must walk into the dark together in order to discover the light.

CHAPTER 9

Want to Lose Belief?
Join the Church

Returning to Where We Came and
Seeing It for the First Time

The previous practices provide some concrete examples
of how one might encourage people to enter into the
rupturing event of Christianity in a communal setting.
By disrupting our master narratives and exposing the
impotence of our Idolatrous pursuit, they invite us into a
different type of existence in which we engage with the
world around us in a different way.

However, entering into and remaining faithful to the
vision outlined thus far is difficult. We are constantly being

told that we can be happy and fulfilled if only we pursue the right dream, make the correct amount of money, look a certain way, buy a particular product, or worship a particular deity. The demand upon our lives is the demand that we should pursue our happiness and fulfillment at all costs. It is then as important as ever that we create clearings where we are invited to give up this vision, spaces where the deception of this demand is exposed and where we can learn simply to be. Where instead of certainty and satisfaction, we can embrace unknowing and celebrate life without the felt need to be complete.

Instead of repressing or disavowing our humanity, we need places where we come to embrace it, returning to where we already were but experiencing it in a different way. This will require the formation of collectives that invite us to leave our cultural, political, and religious views at the door; let go of our frantic pursuits for wholeness; sensitize us to one another; and learn to embrace our lives. Such groups will differ hugely in how they look, but what follows are a few examples of how one collective, ikon, attempted to embody these ideas in liturgical form.

Here I will outline three case studies, each of which was enacted in both a small and large setting. The small setting was a bar in Belfast, Northern Ireland, with around sixty to eighty people, while the large gatherings took place at a festival.

It is worth mentioning that in each of the following case studies other things took place that I have not mentioned. The desire here is simply to draw broad-brush strokes so that the reader can begin to imagine different ways that such liturgical spaces could be enacted. I will not be offering any commentary on these events but instead will let them speak for themselves in much the same way as they would for the people who originally participated in them.

Case Study 1: Fundamentalism

This was the first event that ikon had ever offered in such a large venue. The room was huge and there was only an hour to set up. As the organizers rushed around getting everything ready, a large crowd began to gather at the doors.

In addition to the growing crowd waiting to enter the building, there was another group outside. They were making it very clear that they had no intention of joining us for the gathering; in fact, they were there to warn people against being part of the event.

This group was made up of around fifteen protesters, many armed with banners. They were chanting slogans that denounced ikon as heresy, engaging people in arguments, and handing out tracts written specifically against ikon. Things were tense as many of those waiting to get into the building began to get defensive at the treatment they were receiving. Finally, however, the doors opened and people began to stream inside.

What people didn't know, including the festival organizers, was that the protesters were actually part of the event. They had been placed there as a way of creating an appropriate context for the subject matter of the evening. The event itself sought to explore questions regarding the way we hold beliefs and engage with those who think differently. By providing this foil, we were able to draw out our natural tendency to mirror the aggressive certainty of another by holding even more tightly to what we believe.

Upon entering the room, people were confronted with a large, stark stage upon which five people stood motionless, side by side. The only object on the stage was a large wooden soapbox. Around the room hundreds of pages from a Bible lay crumpled into tight balls, like rocks ready to be thrown. The seating was in rows facing the front to resemble a traditional church environment.

> **Around the room hundreds of pages from a Bible lay crumpled into tight balls, like rocks ready to be thrown.**

Once the room was full, one of the people on the stage stepped forward, stood on the soapbox, and spoke: "Good evening. In the Gospel according to John chapter 14, verse 6 we read, "Jesus saith unto him, I am the way, the truth, and the life: no man cometh unto the Father, but by me."

As he returned to his original place a young man stepped onto the stage and invited everyone to stand and sing with him. He then began to play a contemporary worship song connected loosely with the Bible verse used in the introduction. As the worship leader played, the words were projected onto a huge wall so that people could sing along. But as he reached the second verse the words began to fade and various phrases began to appear over the top of them:

> *I am the truth*
> *Follow me*
> *Be my friend*
> *I shall crush my enemies beneath my feet*
> *I am the way*
> *It is my way or no way*
> *I am the truth*
> *There is no truth for those who would reject me*
> *I am life*
> *There is only death for those who displease me*
> *Love me*
> *Or I will hate you*
> *I am the truth*
> *Follow me*
> *Be my friend*
> *Or I will destroy you*

As these phrases began to appear, the worship song started to take on a somewhat uncanny and oppressive feel. The words that people were singing began to take on a dark meaning that had been absent before.

177

When the musician finished, he placed his guitar on the ground and told everyone that he wanted to share his testimony. He then proceeded to talk about how he had once been a Christian and worship leader but had gradually walked away from his beliefs. He spoke frankly and movingly about his loss of faith and described how the news was received by his friends. The words were deeply personal as he outlined how he had found himself on the outside of the church he had once been part of. In less than five minutes he had brought us all to a place of quiet introspection by describing how his changing view on the world had placed him outside the walls of the community he loved.

As he left the stage, a young woman who had been standing silently in the background stepped forward and stood on the soapbox. She paused for a moment and looked out into the crowd. Then she opened her mouth to speak, but nothing came out. She stammered for a moment, paused, then cleared her throat. But again no sound came from her lips. After a minute or so of this hesitation and silence, she simply hung her head in shame and returned to her spot on the stage. After a few more seconds a page from the Bible appeared on the wall behind her with the words from 1 Corinthians 14 highlighted and underlined:

Women should remain silent in the churches. They are not allowed to speak, but must be in submission, as the Law says.

A few moments later, another woman who had been standing motionless on the stage stepped forward and mounted the soapbox. In contrast to her predecessor she spoke eloquently, delivering a short but deeply moving sermon entitled "The Singing Ministry of Christ." It was a grace-filled reflection that overflowed with the themes of forgiveness and love. But no sooner had she finished than the same sermon began to crackle loudly through speakers set up around the room. This time, however, it was being preached by a man, a man whose distinctive voice most of those gathered instantly recognized. This was the voice of an infamous fundamentalist preacher. As his voice boomed loudly around the room, his image appeared on the various screens while a DJ mixed music beneath his words. Everyone was thus confronted with the fact that this beautiful sermon was written by a figure whom most in the room would have rejected as having little of worth to say.

As the words began to fade, a different musician took to the stage and sang a hymn full of brokenness and humility called "Maranatha" (lyrics of which can be found in *Insurrection*). As he sang this beautiful song of longing, which provided a powerful contrast to the song that opened the gathering, ushers silently moved through the room giving each person a fragment of rice paper with some doctrinal belief written on the surface with food coloring.

At the end of the song a man on the stage took to the soapbox and spoke. He spoke of how our beliefs can so often shield us from one another, protecting us from a real encounter with the people to our right and to our left. He talked about how our ideas of what is true can prevent us from allowing others to be a source of our own growth, and he told a story about how we might allow our beliefs and the beliefs of others to nourish the world rather than destroy it.

When he finished his reflection, a young woman asked us to take a moment to think about our various beliefs. She then invited everyone to turn to the person beside him or her and say, "These are my beliefs, broken for you," before offering that person the rice paper for consumption.

That evening everyone was invited to take home one of the rock-like Bible pages that had been strewn around the room as an aid to further reflection on the night.

Case Study 2: The God Delusion

There were three entrances to the venue on this particular night, each with a large banner: one read, "Believer"; another, "Unbeliever"; and a third read, "Undecided."

> **There were three entrances to the venue labeled "Believer," "Unbeliever," and "Undecided."**

To enter the building people had to decide which door to use, and to make the choice a little more difficult, a rumor had being circulated that the only door that actually led into the event was the one labeled "Unbeliever."

In reality each door led into a lobby where some stalls had been set up that offered various exotic-looking pills and potions. People at each of the stalls were giving those who passed a passionate sales pitch, inviting them to take free samples of their stock and promising that they had a product that would fill the void in life and bring healing to hearts. There were also well-dressed officials walking around the crowd randomly giving out bandages with words like "Faith," "God," "Science," "Nature," "Belief," "Doubt," "Wealth," and "Health" stamped on them, or passing out small vials of liquid with "The solution" typed onto labels on the front.

At the other end of the lobby was a door that led into the main room. Upon entering people were confronted with the sight of a seemingly giant woman standing in the center of the auditorium. She stood eighteen feet tall and wore a huge multicolored woolen dress.

Pieces of yarn stretched from her sprawling dress and crisscrossed the room in all directions, ending up on the knitting needles of people in various locations who were busy making clothes out of the unraveling of this giant dress. In addition, a young woman circled the dress, cutting yarn from the dress into pieces approximately six inches in length.

In contrast to this giant woman, the stage was mostly empty except for a tiny marionette standing approximately two feet high in front of a small black curtain.

A long cable with an old-fashioned bulb on one end was draped from the ceiling so that it hung about six feet above a spot on the stage. It had a small string attached that enabled it to be turned on and off. In addition to this, the Nicene Creed was projected onto various walls. These projections came directly from a computer that sat on an old writing desk.

In addition to this, a woman sitting to one side of the stage was surrounded by hundreds of ornate origami cranes. She was slowly unfolding them.

Once the room was filled with people, a woman stood up and announced that throughout the gathering people could go to the computer on the writing desk and edit the creed, putting words in and taking words out as they saw fit.

A few moments later, a young man walked onto the stage, stood beneath the light bulb, switched it on, and addressed the crowd:

Ladies and Gentlemen, thank you for joining us this evening. Take a seat and make yourselves comfortable. Tonight we would like to share a secret with you, a sacred secret that must be kept strictly between us.

A number of years ago while I was walking home late one evening, I heard a voice from heaven calling my name. I stood still and listened intently to what I took to be nothing less than the voice of God. As I waited, rooted to the spot, God spoke to me.

At this point the giant woman who had been standing silently in the center of the room spoke out: "I do not exist." The man then continued,

It seemed as if I was being confronted with the loss of God instigated by none other than God. I was confused, my world began to spin, and everything that I took to be solid began to melt into thin air. And yet there seemed to be something deeply important about these divine words, something that I am unraveling to this day.

He then switched off the light and a spotlight illuminated the small marionette, which stood up and began to speak:

I would like to tell you the story of a small town filled with believers who sought to act always in obedience to the voice of God. When faced with difficult situations, the leaders of the community would often be found deep in prayer, or searching the scriptures for guidance and wisdom. Late one evening, in the middle of winter, a young man from the neighboring city arrived at the gates of the town's little church seeking refuge. The caretaker immediately let him in and, seeing that he was hungry and cold, provided a meal and some warm clothes. After he had eaten, the young man explained how he had fled the city because the authorities had labeled him a political dissident. It turned out that the man had been critical of both the government and the church in his work as a journalist. The caretaker brought the young man back to his home and allowed him to stay until a plan had been worked out concerning what to do next.

When the priest was informed of what had happened, he called the leaders of the town together in order to work out what ought to be done. After two days of discussion, it was agreed that the man should be handed over to the authorities in order to face up to the crimes he had committed. But the caretaker protested, saying, "This man has committed no crimes; he has merely criticized what he believes to be the injustices perpetrated by authorities in the name of God."

"What you say may be true," replied the priest, "but his presence puts the whole of this town in danger. What if the authorities work out where he is and learn that we protected him?"

But the caretaker refused to hand him over to the priest, saying, "He is my guest, and while under my roof I will ensure that no harm comes to him. If you take him from me by force, then I will publicly attest to having helped him and suffer the same injustice as my guest."

The caretaker was well loved by the people and the priest had no intention of letting something happen to him. So the leaders went away again and this time searched the scriptures for an answer, for they knew that the caretaker was a man of deep faith. After a whole night of poring over the scriptures the leaders came back to the caretaker saying, "We have read the sacred book all through the night seeking guid-

> **The caretaker refused to hand him over to the priest, saying, "He is my guest, and while under my roof I will ensure that no harm comes to him."**

ance and found that it tells us that we must respect the authorities of this land and witness to the truth of faith through submission to them."

But the caretaker also knew the sacred words of scripture and told them that the Bible also asked that we care for those who suffer and are persecuted. There and then the leaders began to pray fervently. They beseeched God to speak to them, not as a still small voice in their conscience, but in the way that He had spoken to Abraham and Moses. They begged that God would communicate directly to them and to the caretaker so that the issue could finally be resolved. Sure enough, the sky began to darken and God descended from heaven, saying, "The priest and elders speak the truth, my friend. In order to protect the town, this man must be handed over to the authorities."

But the caretaker, a man of deep faith, looked up to heaven and replied, "If you want me to remain faithful to you, my God, then I can do nothing but refuse your advice. For I do not need the scriptures or your words to tell me what I ought to do. You have already demanded that I look after this man. You have written that I must protect him at all costs. Your words of love have been spelled out by the lines of this man's face; your text is found in the texture of his flesh. And so my God, I defy you precisely so as to remain faithful to you."

With this God withdrew with a smile, knowing that the matter had finally been settled.*

As this story came to an end, a man quietly stood beneath the dangling light and switched it on. He then put a megaphone to his lips and began to speak:

Where does your faith lie?

Does your faith lie in the belief that the universe was created in six twenty-four-hour days?

Does your faith lie in there being an ark on Mount Ararat?

Does your faith lie in the notion that the next politician you vote for will not support the next war?

Does your faith lie in the hope that heaven is full of people like you?

Does your faith lie in the free market?

Does your faith lie in scientific rationalism?

Does your faith lie in your own ability to discern the mind of God?

---

*Peter Rollins, *The Orthodox Heretic: And Other Impossible Tales* (Brewster, MA: Paraclete Press, 2009), pp. 94–97.

Does your faith lie in your tradition being closer to the truth than another?

Does your faith lie in the virgin birth?

Does your faith lie in a balanced diet and exercising?

Does your faith lie in maintenance of the status quo?

Does your faith lie in your beloved eventually coming to their senses and taking you back?

Does your faith lie in a hell beyond this life for those who didn't accept Jesus Christ?

Does your faith lie in your job?

Does your faith lie in financial savings?

Does your faith lie in liberalism?

Does your faith lie in your own good intentions?

Where does your faith . . .

Where does your faith . . .

Lie?*

His hand dropped to his side, he turned off the light and returned to his seat. At this point the young woman who had been unfolding small origami birds stopped what she was doing and addressed the crowd:

I am trying to learn origami by going backwards. I have stolen a paper crane from the shoebox of junk in the corner and am unfolding it slowly, stopping with each reversing stage to commit the shape and passing landmarks to memory. I quickly discover that it doesn't

---

*This is an edited version of a script written and performed by Jon Hatch.

work. When I reach the beginning of all this unravel-ing, I am forced to accept that, despite its map of lines and creases, what lies before me on the table is just a piece of paper, and I am powerless to turn it back into a bird.*

Someone else joined her, pulling apart one of the ori-gami cranes before speaking:

Here I am unraveling! It began with a doubt. A tickling thread, an element itching. Not much, but at the time I wanted it gone; I prayed for it to disappear.

Unraveling. Some early questions coming out of the fray: How can I claim to know God? How can I comfortably address Infinite-God in prayer? What is my faith made of?

This doubt was mocking me: "You live your family inheritance! You've invested so much you can't let it go! Your identity is tied up in Christendom—pull this thread and you will be nothing!" Mocking little dan-gling thread of doubt.

The thread. I couldn't ignore the itch. Should I snip it off and pretend it never existed? Or should I pull it and examine my reasons for belief? I decided I would pull it until it stopped. My faith would find its form and still keep me warm. It would stand up to the test.

---

*Written and performed by Kellie Turtle.

I would tug this thread and come out stronger. . . . I came out weaker.

Every question led to another. Each answer was teased apart, showing its own presuppositions. Every new experience I was open to and every stranger I met pulled at the thread. I was unraveling, and I was unraveling fast. What would be left?

Filled with doubt! Filled with failure! Filled with uncertainty!

That's how it started, this unraveling.

But unraveling and raveling, I was both. They mean the same thing. I started to see that unraveling didn't need the negative appendage, the un- prefix. As if unraveling were to be avoided, to be considered the ruin of my belief, as if this dissection indicated the death of my faith.

My Christ-encounter had become meshed in interpretation and tangled in my inheritance (church, theology, psychology, politics). My "becoming-Christ" had become "Christian" (in all its woolen glory). But instead of unraveling these threads to expose an embarrassed belief, this raveling disentangles the web of confusing adornments and décor to make room for the next encounter.

Raveling. Disentangling, not collapsing. My faith didn't unravel, it raveled. They mean the same thing. I learned to revel in raveling. The questions proclaim more than the answers. The searching confirms that there has been revelation. The hunt for an unattainable treasure confirms that we have found it. Tearing apart what I love is evidence that I love it.

Forever doubting! Forever failing! Forever uncertain!

I am raveling.*

> Raveling.
> Disentangling, not collapsing. My faith didn't unravel, it raveled.

A woman who was previously knitting then stood up and addressed everyone:

Things come apart. The center cannot hold.

As soon as I was knit together in my mother's womb, I began to unravel.

I remember the exact moment of my undoing. The moment where I realized that all my answers had to change because I had changed.

I was lying in bed. A few days before a human being had burst out of my body into a room full of strangers. For months she had lived, meditating inside me, whispering that she had the final answer and would tell me soon. And now she came out and split me open and split everything apart.

The center cannot hold.

So later I lay in bed and suddenly realized everything I didn't know and would never know. Suddenly

---

*Written and performed by Stephen Caswell.

realized that I did not know God. And as I thought that most terrifying of thoughts, he left me.

God left me.

Things come apart.

The god with the answers was gone. The god with my security was gone. The god with my future, secretly stored until the appointed time of its revelation, was gone. The godman who promised to never leave. The god who was my father. The god who was not my father. The god who spoke my personality. The god who wrote my behavior down like a map. The god who told me the code to decipher the whole world and all its mysteries—space and time, life and death, holy and profane—was gone.

And I was gone, unraveled completely, from the soul out.

But we do not see things as they are; we see them as we are. And I suddenly saw myself, someone who had been unraveling since the time I had been knit together in my own mother's womb. As soon as I was born, I started to look for the answer to the question that was birthed in my beginning. From the moment of my birth, trying to reknit myself and remember, remember god. But I never could do it. There always were those questions. I ignored them because I wanted the answer so badly. And I forgot that there is no answer without the question. Perhaps the best we can do is observe our unique unraveling and the way in which we survive it. I am this creature, continually coming apart, but I was born to do it. I am in the unraveling and the making new and the tearing down and the building up again, I am in the question and continually . . .

in the question.

And it is now my observation that my god is in the business of unraveling. God is not keeping me all together, wrapped up in swaddling clothes to keep me safe or bandages to hold me in or a shroud to mask my death. Because the only real safety is in death. And I was born to unravel myself down the path of life towards life.*

As a joint liturgy, the Nicene Creed that had been edited by people throughout the gathering was read aloud by anyone who wanted to participate:

I believe that creeds aren't worth the paper they are written on . . . But I still believe in God.

I believe that if you look at my life, you'll only sometimes see what I believe.

I believe that if we have two coats, we should give one away (though I don't do it).

Today I don't believe in anything; tomorrow who knows.

I sometimes believe in God—one who existed before time, beyond gender or fathom.

---

*Written and performed by Shirley-Anne McMillan.

Maker of heaven and earth and ginger (all good things), whales, two-hundred-foot cliffs, cloud banks, shipwrecks,

And in Jesus Christ, God's only Son our Lord,

Who was conceived by the Holy Ghost—how?

Born of a fourteen-year-old, Mary, scared out of her wits

Was crucified, dead, and buried, and I used to believe in the penal substitution theory of atonement, but now I just see a violent death and struggle to see how violence can ever be redemptive . . .

He descended into hell, or was hell all around him all the time?

The third day he rose again from the dead.

He ascended into safety of abstraction, away from having to feel this, from dealing with this,

And sits, maybe sprawls, on the right hand of God the Father Almighty.

I believe in me; I believe in the Spirit, Sophia, wisdom . . .

The holy catholic (i.e., everybody) Church;

The Communion of saints; does this mean me?

LOVE

The Forgiveness of sins (but I still feel shame); (don't you?)

The Resurrection of the body.

I believe in singing the body electric

And the life everlasting,

A life we find right here in our midst

Threads that had been cut from the dress of the giant woman were distributed by ushers who said, "Pull yourself apart," while tying them around people's wrists. As this was happening, the marionette told a final story:

There is an ancient Jewish parable that speaks of a heated debate taking place in a park between two old and learned rabbis. The conversation in question revolves around a particularly complex and obscure verse in the Torah. It is not the first time that these two intellectual giants have crossed swords over this verse; in fact, they have debated it for years, sometimes changing their opinions but never finding a consensus. God is, of course, known to have the patience of a saint, but even God begins to tire of the endless discussion. So finally God decides to visit the two men and tell them once and for all what the parable means. God reaches down, pulls the clouds apart, and begins to speak, "You have been debating this verse endlessly for years; I will now tell you what it means," but before God could continue, the two rabbis look up and say, in a rare moment of unity, "Who are you to tell us what the verse means? You have given us the words, now leave us in peace to wrestle with it."

To close, a benediction written and performed by Pádraig Ó Tuama was offered, entitled "Go in Pieces."*

---

*This benediction can be found in my book *Insurrection*.

Case Study 3: Pyro-theology

Outside the venue some stewards with clipboards and yellow safety jackets strolled up and down the crowd to ascertain if people were entering the auditorium with anything flammable, telling off people who were not carrying lighters, matches, or dangerous liquids.

Once through the doors everyone had to walk along a short blacked-out corridor with a fire alarm sounding and a woman's voice repeating, "There is a fire inside the building, please remain calm and step inside." On the other side, people were given a page from a religious text that was being ripped out of a book at random.

Small unlit bonfires lay dotted around the room, while a large funeral pyre stood at the front with five people on top of it, blindfolded and wearing burnt clothing.

> "There is a fire inside the building, please remain calm and step inside."

A version of the song "This Little Light of Mine" played as people found a place to sit.

A huge image of a burning church filled the wall behind the funeral pyre, while a man positioned on a smaller stage was quietly attempting to set alight a large Bible with flint and some kindling.

As the music began to fade the first person on the funeral pyre picked up a large old book and began to read from it, though he did not remove his blindfold:

Just as it was written by those prophets of old, the last days of the earth overflowed with suffering and pain. In those dark days, a huge pale horse rode through the earth with Death upon its back and Hell in its wake. During this great tribulation, the earth was scorched with the fires of war, rivers ran red with blood, the soil withheld its fruit, and disease descended like a mist. One by one all the nations of the earth were brought to their knees.

Far from all the suffering, high up in the heavenly realm, God watched the events unfold with a heavy heart. An ominous silence had descended upon heaven as the angels witnessed the earth being plunged into darkness and despair. But this could only continue for so long, for at the designated time, God stood upright, breathed deeply, and addressed the angels, "The time has now come for me to separate the sheep from the goats, the healthy wheat from the inedible chaff."

Having spoken these words, God slowly turned to face the world and called forth to the church with a booming voice, "Rise up and ascend to heaven all of you who have sought to escape the horrors of this world by sheltering beneath my wing. Come to me all who have turned from this suffering world by calling out 'Lord, Lord.'"

In an instant, millions were caught up in the clouds and ascended into the heavenly realm, leaving the suffering world behind them.

Once this great rapture had taken place, God paused for a moment and then addressed the angels, saying, "It is done, I have separated the people born of my spirit from those who have turned from me. It is time now for us to leave this place and take up residence in the earth, for it is there that we shall find our people: the ones who would forsake heaven in order to embrace the earth, the few who would turn away from eternity itself to serve at the feet of a fragile, broken life that passes from existence in but an instant."

And so it was that God and the heavenly host left that place to dwell among those who had rooted themselves upon the earth—the ones who had forsaken God for the world and thus who bore the mark of God; the few who had discovered heaven in the very act of forsaking it.*

As he finished a well-dressed man walked onto the stage and began to speak:

These are the words of Saint Cosmas of Aetolia. If you want to find perfect love, go sell all your belongings, give them to the poor, go where you find a master and become a slave. Can you do this and be perfect?

He then left the stage while a musician began to sing, mixing Christian hymns with popular songs dealing with the theme of fire.

When she finished, the man who had previously quoted the words of Saint Cosmas took to the stage again;

---

*Peter Rollins, *Insurrection* (New York: Howard, 2011), pp. 137–139.

this time his clothes were slightly charred. Once more he began to speak:

> If you want to find perfect love, go sell all your belongings, give them to the poor, go where you find a master and become a slave. Can you do this and be perfect? You say this is too heavy? Then do something else. Don't sell yourself as a slave. Just sell your belongings and give them all to the poor. Can you do it? Or do you find this too heavy a task?

Again he hung his head and left the stage while another person from the pyre began to speak. She spoke passionately of the child abuse scandal that rocked the Catholic church in Ireland from the 1970s to the dawn of the twenty-first century and the church's various attempts to cover the facts up.

When she had finished, the man who had quoted Saint Cosmas returned to the stage, only this time his clothes were very burnt. Again he addressed all those present:

> If you want to find perfect love, go sell all your belongings, give them to the poor, go where you find a master and become a slave. Can you do this and be perfect? You say this is too heavy? Then do something else. Don't sell yourself as a slave. Just sell your belongings and give them all to the poor. Can you do it? Or do you find this too heavy a task? All right, you cannot give away all

your belongings. Then give half, or a third, or a fifth. Is even this too heavy? Then give one-tenth. Can you do that? Is it still too heavy?

> You say this is too heavy? Then do something else. Don't sell yourself as a slave. Just sell your belongings and give them all to the poor.

When he had finished, he looked out at all those gathered, as if waiting for a response, before shaking his head and leaving.

This was followed by some poetry, music, and personal reflections from those on the funeral pyre on the theme of fire.

Once more the man quoting Saint Cosmas returned to the stage, this time with clothes that were almost entirely burnt. Again he addressed those gathered:

If you want to find perfect love, go sell all your belongings, give them to the poor, go where you find a master and become a slave. Can you do this and be perfect? You say this is too heavy? Then do something else. Don't sell yourself as a slave. Just sell your belongings and give them all to the poor. Can you do it? Or do you find this too heavy a task? All right, you cannot give away all your belongings. Then give half, or a third, or a fifth. Is even this too heavy? Then give one-tenth. Can you do that? Is it still too heavy? How about this. Don't sell yourself as a slave. Don't give a penny to the poor. Only do this. Don't take your poor brother's coat, don't take his bread, don't persecute him, don't eat him alive. If you don't want to do him any good, at least do him no harm. Just leave him alone. Is this also too heavy? You say you want to be saved. But how? How can we be saved if everything we are called to do is too heavy? We descend and descend until there is no place farther down.*

Again he waited for a few moments in silence before leaving. After some silence one of the people on the funeral pyre removed her blindfold and led everyone in a call and response liturgy on the theme of burning away the old to make room for the new.

The response during this liturgy was not words but the crinkling of the paper that everyone was given at the beginning. When the leader spread her arms, everyone in the room who found himself or herself between the leader's right and left arm was instructed to crinkle the paper. The higher her arms the louder the noise they were to create. This allowed the leader to control the sound, creating a wave of rustling that moved across the room that sounded like a fire.

After this time of call and response, everyone was encouraged to go to one of the bonfires and place his or her page into it as a sign that all our religious narratives are but ash before the all-consuming fire of divine mystery.

At the end a fire alarm signaled that it was time to

---

*http://www.comeandseeicons.com/c/phn56.htm.

leave. At the exits stewards handed out books of matches while instructing people to go start a fire.

Go Start a Fire

This final section has attempted to outline some concrete ways that one group has tried to invite, explore, and live out the ideas explored here by liturgically enacting the new creation. There are countless churches that sell us a false promise of certainty and satisfaction, millions of temples around the globe built in honor of those insidious Idols. In contrast, there are a few insurrectionary groups that are seriously attempting to explore what it might mean to give up the idea of God as a product, dissident voices calling us to live fully in this world with an embrace of our unknowing.

If you look you might be fortunate enough to find such groups in your area, or perhaps you are already a part of such a collective. But if not, then you may need to start one. As yet there are few churches from which to gain an apprenticeship and even fewer seminaries equipped to train you. So you may need to venture out alone, walking a dark road with little or no support. It won't be easy, and it is very likely that anything you do try will fail. But try you must, and keep trying.

I hope you will think of this book as a box of matches and these closing words as a plea to go and start some fires of your own. Fires that will burn away the Idols we so tightly hold on to, fires that will melt away the false certainties that we clothe ourselves in, fires that will keep us warm as we go about the difficult task of facing up to our anxieties, accepting the mystery of life, and embracing the world in love.

> I hope you will think of this book as a box of matches and these closing words as a plea to go and start some fires of your own.

A Faith Full of
Signs and Wonders

There was once a poor and quiet woman who lived in one of the world's largest cities. She was a gentle soul who worked tirelessly with those in need. In her spare time she would paint and often subsidized her work by sketching the portraits of wealthy tourists as they walked through the streets in their fine robes.

In the evening she would often be found sitting in one the local taverns, talking with friends and strangers before returning to her humble apartment on the edge of the city.

Her life continued in this way for many years until one day she made an incredible discovery. She found that she had been bestowed with an amazing ability. She found that she could perform great, magical feats of the sort only spoken of in fables. One word from her lips was enough to generate great wealth, and a mere thought could transform her little home into a palace.

It was not long before her fame spread throughout the land. Once word of this woman's gift had begun to circulate, people began to visit her from far-off places, often traveling thousands of miles just to sit in her presence. Soon even those in power began to take note of this miracle worker and were challenged by what she did.

Yet throughout her entire life not one person ever learned of her magical powers, for never once did she use them. She could have taken herself out of the city in an instant. She could have transformed her life in the blink of an eye. Yet she did not need to, for she loved her life and saw it as already infused with such intense beauty and meaning.

Instead people began to take notice of her because of her supernatural work among the poor and oppressed. Never before had they encountered someone who could love so selflessly and forgive so naturally. They were seduced by her life because this gentle woman had learned to give without seeking return, to love without reserve and to live with joy.

The people were so poor that they longed to be in the presence of one who knew how to embrace life in all of its beauty and horror, someone who was able to smile deeply, embrace suffering, celebrate the cycle of life and accept the inevitability of death. This woman's very life was her miracle and her example was her gift to humanity.

The rich were so poor that they longed to be in the presence of one who knew how to embrace life in all of its beauty and horror.

Acknowledgments

Like a genealogy, these names trace the bloodline of the book. Without them it would not exist in the form that it does. First and foremost my thanks go to the Olson Foundation for believing that I might have something to say and offering the support that has allowed the time and space to find out; to Brian and Jill, whose generosity and kindness knows no bounds; and to Greg Daniel and Andy Meisenheimer, who were so directly involved in the book's publication.

The ideas that went into constructing this work were extracted from multiple thinkers. Their fingerprints are to be found all over these pages, to be discovered by detectives who wish to scan the scene of the crime and work out who should be held responsible. To make the job a little easier, the work of Jacques Lacan, Slavoj Žižek, Bruce Fink, Paul Hessert and Frederiek Depoortere have proved formative in its construction.

Finally, if you are someone who seeks to engage critically with these ideas, wrestle with them, and put them into practice, then I thank you. Without those who are willing to engage, critique, and flesh out these ideas in the formation of new collectives, these words are empty.

READING GROUP GUIDE

THE IDOLATRY OF GOD
PETER ROLLINS

Introduction

Is God just another product on the market, promising the elusive happiness and satisfaction we crave? In *The Idolatry of God*, theological firebrand Peter Rollins asserts that a deep existential conflict exists between people who are willing to embrace doubt and uncertainty in matters of faith, and those who cling to certainty—who make an idol of God. To close this gap, Rollins invites us all to take a hard look at our most cherished beliefs, to approach truth in bold new ways, and to embrace a faith that throws us into the world rather than shielding us from it.

Topics and Questions for Discussion

1. Reflect on the book's title, *The Idolatry of God*. What thoughts and/or questions does the title raise in your mind?

2. In the Introduction the author writes that his book is about the theme of salvation, saying that this is "not the type of salvation that is preached today from the pulpit, the false salvation that promises us freedom from our unknowing and dissatisfaction, but a salvation that takes places *within* our unknowing and dissatisfaction. One that directly confronts them, embraces them, and says 'amen' to them." Is this a new idea for you? Do you find it comforting? Disturbing? Neutral? Discuss this idea, drawing on your own experiences of faith and belief.

3. Do you sense that there is a "gap" in your being, dating back to infancy? If so, describe what that gap feels like for you. What is the source of this gap, according to the author?

4. Discuss the MacGuffin and how it is depicted in various movies and books. Do you cling to any personal MacGuffins?

5. In Chapter 1 the author defines Original Sin as the gap in the core of our being. Compare this definition to what you believe or were taught about Original Sin. Which definition seems most reasonable? Why? Also consider the author's explanations of Total Depravity and the Law and how they fit, or don't fit, with what you have been taught.

6. What is an Idol? What purpose does it serve? Provide a few examples of an Idol.

7. In Chapter 2 Rollins outlines three strategies used to avoid a confrontation with our pain: deferment, repression, and disavowal. Is this something you think has resonance for you? Do you typically default to one of these strategies? If so, which one and why?

8. In Chapter 3 the author reflects on four coping responses—consumption, vomiting, tolerance, and agreement—that we use to protect ourselves from the disturbing effect of encountering someone with a different worldview than our own. Have you used any of these in your own life?

9. What is "literalistic listening"? Give some examples of literalistic listening in action. Think of a conversation you've had (or witnessed) recently. Might the conversation have taken a different course if one or both parties had employed literalistic listening? Explain.

10. According to the author, how does modern Christianity resemble a zombie apocalypse? Do you agree or disagree with this assertion? Why?

11. What does it mean to call the Crucifixion "the sacrifice of sacrifice itself"? How might accepting this approach affect the life of the Christian, as compared to more traditional conservative or liberal approaches?

12. Explain what the author means by the Paulinian cut or Paulinian universalism. Have you experienced the Paulinian cut in your own life? If so, describe the experience. What tribes were you separated from? What tribes did you move toward?

13. In what way(s) can an "addiction to certainty" pose a problem for the Christian? Do you agree that it is a problem in the church today? Why or why not?

15. In Chapter 6, Rollins imagines God whispering to a doubting believer, "It's okay, you don't have to stop believing in me; I have stopped believing in myself." What does this mean? Share your reactions. Discuss some ways in which the true God differs from the Idol introduced earlier.

16. What did you hope to learn or experience by reading this book? Were your expectations fulfilled?

Enhance Your Book Club

1. Within your group, practice literalistic listening as described in Chapter 3. Imagine a few potentially heated conversations. Invite two volunteers to demonstrate this imaginary conversation using non-literalistic listening. Then do it again with one or both participants demonstrating literalistic listening. In what ways did the two conversations differ? Discuss some practical ways your group can practice literalistic listening in your daily lives.

2. Summarize each of the following "Dis-Courses" and describe the purposes of each:

   - The Last Supper
   - The Evangelism Project
   - Atheism for Lent
   - Omega Course

   Why does the author emphasize that these events should be experienced in community rather than alone?

3. What do you think about introducing these or other kinds of Dis-Courses within your group or community? Discuss various "tribes" that might be involved. Choose an idea and plan some action steps for making it happen.

4. In Chapter 9 the author describes three ikon case studies: Fundamentalism, The God Delusion, and Pyro-theology. Discuss the elements included in these events and your reactions to them. Can you envision introducing similar elements into your own faith community? Why or why not?

5. What might such a collective experience look like in your community? As a group, brainstorm some possibilities. What might be the theme, and why? What impact would you hope the event would have on the community?

6. When you've finished brainstorming, share whatever thoughts and feelings came up during the process. Did you find the exercise easy or difficult? Did envisioning this type of collective experience make you feel optimistic? Pessimistic? Anxious? Hopeful? All of the above? Why?

7. If your group favors the idea of organizing a collective gathering, think of some practical ways that you, as an individual and as a group, could help bring it about. Where could a gathering be held? Who would attend and why? What kinds of songs would be sung or music played? Is there a specific action that you can take this month? This week? Today?

A Conversation with Peter Rollins

Can you discuss the title, The Idolatry of God, *and how it relates to the central question of your book?*

It is becoming more and more popular today for people in the church to avoid specifically theological language in their conversations and writings. You see this take place, for instance, in the ongoing creation of Bible translations that aim at a text written in "plain language." In contrast to this trend, I am interested in returning to, rethinking, and reengaging with many of these ancient theological notions. This is because I believe that these terms possess a depth, potency, and weight which we have barely touched upon, an incendiary force that goes far beyond the facile understanding of the terms we so often find preached by religionists.

The central term that I wish to explore and open up in this book is idolatry. More specifically, I want to show how the idea of God today preached within much of the church is nothing more than an impotent Idol. Simply stated, this boils down to the claim that God is treated as nothing more than a product, a product that promises certainty and satisfaction while delivering nothing but deception and dissatisfaction.

This might be a bold claim, but it gets to the heart of my theological project. By grasping this the reader will understand what I mean when I claim that the actually existing church broadly represents the old creation, along with my argument that a new collective is possible, a collective that exists beyond idolatry. A collective that can cross tribal boundaries, teach us how to embrace the world, and fight for real emancipation.

What factors inspired or compelled you to write The Idolatry of God *at this time? Do you feel it contains a message of particular significance "for such a time as this" in the history of the church?*

All of my books are written in an attempt to speak into and identify the core issue that we must wrestle with in order to birth a new and vibrant community grounded in the liberating message found in the event of Christ. My books and writing seek to find that Archimedean point from which we can overturn the mammoth structure that propagates a reactionary and idolatrous form of life in the false guise of Christian faith; a structure that we might mock with our minds, but which we embrace at a liturgical and material level. This latest book is my most systematic and clear presentation of the problem as I envision it. In this way I believe that it offers the interpretive key from which all my other work can be understood. It represents the enclosure within which the rest of my work rests.

What specific trends or characteristics of the modern church do you seek to counteract with this book? What changes do you hope to see in areas of worship, ministry, and community?

Basically I argue that the modern church engages in a host of material practices designed to act as a security blanket for life. It does this by offering preaching, prayers and songs that solidify our tribal identities and promise fulfillment. In so doing the church becomes a type of crack house selling feel-good drugs to those who enter its doors. The problem, however, is that our attempt to avoid the inherent difficulties of life does not mean that we are free from suffering but rather that we are most oppressed by it. The truth that we suffer might be one that we can avoid much of the time, but we are always in danger of being directly confronted with it. Because of this we tend to cling to a security blanket, whether it is church, drink, or drugs.

Such acts are not in themselves a problem but rather the solution to a problem—namely, the problem of pain. Yet the limitation of this solution is exposed the next day when we experience the return of everything we had repressed. The pain is not worked through but simply avoided. As a result we are tempted to repeat the cycle.

There is, however, a different way to approach our pain. This other way involves participation in symbolic activity. For example, you might go to hear a poet who puts into music the suffering of loss, an individual who is able to speak the type of suffering you feel in lyrical form. In such a poet we encounter an individual who has demonstrated profound courage, for in being able to sing her suffering she shows that she is not overwrought by it. As we listen to the music we are invited to touch the dark core of the music so as to encounter our own dark core in a way that we can handle.

My concern is that most of the actually existing church acts as a type of drug den with the leaders being like the nicest, most sincere drug dealers. What we pay for are songs, sermons, and prayers that help us avoid our suffering rather than work through it.

In contrast I am arguing for collectives that are more like the professional mourners who cry for us in a way that confronts us with our own suffering, the stand-up comedians who talk about the pain of being human, or the poets singing about life at the local pub.

In other words, a church where the liturgical structure does not treat God as a product that would make us whole but as the mystery that enables us to live abundantly in the midst of life's difficulties. A place where we are invited to confront the reality of our humanity, not so that we will despair, but so that we will be free of the despair that already lurks within us, the despair that enslaves us, the despair that we refuse to acknowledge.

What kind of resistance have you received from the religious establishment as a result of the views expressed in The Idolatry of God, *and how do you respond to these critiques?*

Resistance is an interesting phenomenon, as it is different from mere disagreement. There are plenty of people who will disagree with me, many of whom I count as my closest friends. However, there are occasions in which I encounter a type of venomous disagreement that we might term "resistance." What is interesting about this is the way that this response often signals the very opposite of genuine disagreement. Resistance arises whenever a person feels some deep inner conflict over what has been said. This conflict is often the re-sult of some kind of internal clash in which they resonate with what they hear but are unable or unwilling to express that. Strange as it might intially sound, people who show the most resistance to what I am saying often are doing so because what I am saying makes the most sense to them.

Generally I find that people are willing to acknowledge this inner conflict and work through it as long as I approach them in a nonantagonistic, friendly way. In fact some of the people who have attacked me most vigorously in the past have subsequently become friends.

Because of the unsettling nature of my work, I often think that if you have no resistance to the ideas I explore you are not engag-

ing with them seriously enough. I know that I still have resistance
to them.

*Which of your ideas seem to have ignited the most controversy within
Christianity? Why do you think that is?*
Some people have been unnerved by the way that I bracket out certain questions, beliefs, and debates that many in the church take to
be central. By "bracketing out" I am referring to the academic craft
in which one places certain questions to the side in order to address
more basic and potentially important ones. While the church and
its most vocal opponents have tended to focus on issues to do with
the existence of God, the historicity of the various doctrines, and
questions related to the status of the Bible, I am primarily concerned
with the meaning of the Christian event described by the apostle
Paul and what mode of life it expresses. In addition to that I am
concerned with how we enter into that life and express it.

Have you received feedback on the ideas contained in The Idolatry of
God *from people outside of the Christian fold, including atheists and people
of other faiths? If so, what reactions have you received from them, and how
have you responded?*
Yes. Indeed, my primary inspiration for writing the book came as a
direct result of sharing the ideas with some people who would not
describe themselves as theistic or religious. They had not known
that there was such a thing as a faith that genuinely embraced unknowing, celebrated difference and encouraged a direct embrace
of life. Indeed, as I speak across the country, I am discovering that
more and more people from no religious background are engaging
directly with this Christian vision. In addition to this I am find-

ing myself in more conversations with people of various religious traditions (Buddhist, Jewish, Hindu, Muslim, and Christian). Ideas such as the letting go of tribal identity, embracing the world rather than running from it, and rejecting systems that make snake-oil promises of knowing and fulfillment are finding resonance in all sorts of places. Perhaps because these themes are larger than any one religion and prove important to all those interested in what it means to be human.

On a personal note, did the process of writing this book uncover any surprises for you, or take you down a path you didn't expect?
One of the reasons why I so enjoy writing is because of the way that it takes you to places you never imagined when starting off on the journey. Once a book is finished, authors often talk as if they always knew the vantage point that they would get to, but the adventure of writing is much more anarchic than that. If a writer starts with a strong idea of where he will end up and then lands there, he is likely to be engaged in mere dogmatic work rather than the perilous and exciting work of real thinking.

I didn't initially think that I would write a book that so strongly employed theological language. This was not my original intention. I simply wanted to explore what it means to be human and how we might embrace life fully. However, as I wrote, I couldn't get past the provocative resources of the Christian tradition, even though I needed to do a lot of work in order to rescue them from the snatches of the church. As someone who would never have had any intension of writing what academics call a systematic theology, this is what began to take shape as I explored the contours of the landscape I was traversing.

What is the primary message you hope readers will take away from The Idolatry of God?

My main desire is that this work would help to agitate and disturb the reader in a positive way. Rather than simply agreeing or dis-agreeing with the message my hope is that those who engage with the book would find themselves reflecting upon their lives in new and beneficial ways. While there is a part of most writers that gains enjoyment from convincing people to see the world in the way that they do, my primary desire is not in getting people to agree with my vision of the world, but rather to give them a work that encourages them to ask difficult questions of themselves.

My main concern is not is changing what people believe but in asking readers to reflect upon why they believe what they believe. I am inviting people to engage in a type of archaeological dig aimed at discovering if their beliefs are protecting them from the embrace of unknowing and suffering, and if so, what ought to be done about it. Finally, for those readers who find that they are questioning some of the things that they once took for granted, I hope the book will en-courage them to seek out like-minded people who are on the same journey. Individuals who might become fellow workers in the task of forging the new collectives hinted at within the Christian text.

What would you say to the reader who is challenged by The Idolatry of God *and wonders what is the next step in accepting uncertainty and doubt concerning matters of faith as integral to the Christian faith?*

Sometimes I find myself hoping that readers will be unconvinced by what I say or treat it as relatively unimportant. For then they can engage with it in a critical way or read it in a purely recreational way. For those who think that there is something to what I'm saying will find a difficult path stretching before them. If they are a part of some faith community, they might have to ask some difficult questions, questions that will likely be perceived as a threat to the organism. Alternatively the reader might feel convinced to start one of the contemplative practices mentioned in the third section, or even to attempt the creation of a collective which helps people to embrace mystery, unknowing and dissatisfaction. None of this is easy and there are few models available to help, let alone a structure of financial support. It will take the brave, the committed, and the stupid. But the foolishness required to actually try something may just turn out to be wiser than the wisdom of the world.

Do you have another book project in the works?
Yes, I actually have a few. Every time I write I think I have said all that I can, but then every book I write opens up more questions than it answers and reveals new paths that lead into strange, exotic new territories. I can't wait to see where this next one leads.

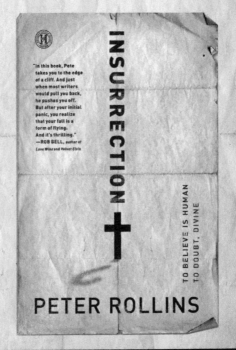